Intercultural Communication

Susan Eckert

**Advance Career & Professional Development
Consulting, Coaching, & Corporate Training
New York**

THOMSON
SOUTH-WESTERN

Australia · Canada · Mexico · Singapore · Spain · United Kingdom · United States

Intercultural Communication, Susan Eckert

VP/Editorial Director:
Jack W. Calhoun

VP/Editor-in-Chief:
Karen Schmohe

Acquisitions Editor:
Jane Phelan

Project Manager:
Dr. Inell Bolls

Consulting Editor:
Andrea Edwards

VP/Director of Marketing:
Carol Volz

Marketing Manager:
Valerie A. Lauer

Marketing Coordinator:
Georgianna Wright

Production Editor:
Kim Kusnerak

Production Manager:
Tricia Matthews Boies

Manufacturing Coordinator:
Kevin Kluck

Art Director:
Tippy McIntosh

Photography Manager:
John Hill

Production House:
Navta Associates, Inc.

Cover Designer:
Joseph Pagliaro Design

Internal Designer:
Tippy McIntosh

Cover Illustration:
Punchstock.com

Photo Researcher:
Rose Alcorn

Printer:
Edwards Brothers
Ann Arbor, MI

For more information contact
Thomson Higher Education
5191 Natorp Boulevard
Mason, Ohio 45040
USA

Or you can visit our Internet site at: http://www.swlearning.com

ASIA (including India)
Thomson Learning
5 Shenton Way
#01-01 UIC Building
Singapore 068808

AUSTRALIA/NEW ZEALAND
Thomson Learning Australia
102 Dodds Street
Southbank, Victoria 3006
Australia

LATIN AMERICA
Thomson Learning
Seneca, 53
Colonia Polanco
11560 Mexico
D.F.Mexico

CANADA
Thomson Nelson
1120 Birchmount Road
Toronto, Ontario
Canada M1K 5G4

UK/EUROPE/MIDDLE
EAST/AFRICA
Thomson Learning
High Holborn House
50-51 Bedford Road
London WC1R 4LR
United Kingdom

SPAIN (includes Portugal)
Thomson Paraninfo
Calle Magallanes, 25
28015 Madrid, Spain

Tools for Workplace Success from Thomson South-Western

NEW! *Human Relations, 3e*
Dalton, Hoyle, and Watts • 0-538-43878-9
This new edition connects students with the human relations issues and challenges they will encounter in the workplace and prepares them to confidently put proven theory into action—so they get the results they want. The authors use a unique approach that provides an opportunity to experience and analyze firsthand the contemporary issues of human relations in the twenty-first century. By weaving their varied professional backgrounds and knowledge into every chapter, they provide the insight and awareness that comes only from experience.

NEW! *Administrative Office Management, Complete Course, 13e*
Odgers • 0-538-43857-6
This text provides the most up-to-date information reflecting contemporary management thinking, issues, and trends that every office employee needs to know. The text provides a strong management-based background while utilizing a humanistic approach for managing and supervising staff in an office environment. A short course text is also available.

NEW! *Connections: Writing for Your World*
Humphrey and Conklin • 0-538-72750-0
This is the only composition text/CD package that continually and systematically connects writing to the real world and the workplace. The writing process is emphasized, paying special attention to methods of organizing, revising, and editing. By focusing on paragraph and essay writing, *Connections* builds basic writing skills that are essential in today's business world.

Business Applications with Microsoft Word
VanHuss, Forde, and Woo • 0-538-72549-4
This text/CD takes document processing out of the classroom and into the workplace. A simulated company serves as the overall structure for this one-of-a-kind text. Realistic workplace projects integrate business vocabulary, critical-thinking strategies, and web-research skills into the instruction of document processing. Workplace themes—such as leadership, ethics, and customer service—are included in each project.

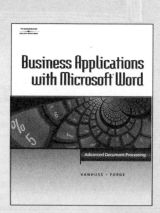

THOMSON
SOUTH-WESTERN

Join us on the Internet at www.swlearning.com

Contents

Preface

A New Critical Competency

Intercultural Communication is more than just a book. It is a comprehensive resource designed to support you in the development of an increasingly critical life skill. Census figures paint a portrait of an increasingly diverse future America, but the future is now. Current workplace demographics already highlight significant changes. At the same time, an increasingly global marketplace is opening new doors—the possibility of conducting business abroad and marketing services and products to new customers with unique needs and interests.

These changes point to the inevitability of greater intercultural interaction. Given the importance of interpersonal effectiveness in professional and business success and the challenges inherent in intercultural communication, the workshops contained in this book are designed to guide you toward greater interpersonal and intercultural effectiveness.

Purpose of This Book

This book will help you:

1. Develop a greater awareness of your multicultural environment and your own cultural worldview

   ➤ Workshop 1: Making Connections

   ➤ Workshop 2: Deconstructing Culture

   ➤ Workshop 3: Learning About Mental Models

2. Build the skills that support effective intercultural interactions

   ➤ Workshop 4: Establishing Key Communication Skills

   ➤ Workshop 5: Making Conversations Work

   ➤ Workshop 6: Learning the Art of Constructive Feedback

   ➤ Workshop 7: Bridging Through Conflict

3. Plan for ongoing learning and integration

   ➤ Workshop 8: Planning for Change and Personal Evolution

Organization of Workshops

Each Workshop includes 1) an opening vignette that illustrates the key points addressed in the Workshop, 2) four different types of activities and exercises to enhance learning, 3) a Workshop summary, and 4) a resource list for further reading and research.

Key Features

Vignette opens each Workshop with a real-world thought-provoking scenario.

Pre-Assessment offers the reader an opportunity to access his/her current knowledge base about the topic.

Goals provided to outline the main objectives of each Workshop.

Quotations used to generate interest and add to thought processes.

Sidebars include added information to enhance learning.

Case Studies offer a window of value-added reality to key concepts presented.

Endnotes provide a list of resources used for each Workshop.

Activities include technology and provide learning opportunities that reinforce and expand on key points.

Figures used in some Workshops to explain a point or provide additional learning for the reader.

Points to Remember used at the end of each Workshop to summarize key ideas presented.

Resources for Facilitators

An Instructor's Resource CD (IRCD) includes supplemental information for each Workshop: facilitator guidelines/lesson plans, PowerPoint slides, a quiz, and solutions to the quiz and Workshop activities and assessments.

About the Author

Susan Eckert has a lifetime of experience in building effective intercultural skills. Her multicultural background has required constant interaction across many different cultures. She has traveled extensively within the United States and has also explored international cultures.

As a professional development consultant, trainer, and coach, Susan has worked with a wide range of organizations, including higher education, non-profit, corporate, dot.com, and "Big 6" firm environments. She holds a BA in Psychology and an MA in Organizational Psychology from Columbia University. Her business Web site can be accessed at www.susaneckert.com.

Acknowledgments

I offer a hearty thanks to each colleague who devoted his/her time, attention, and feedback and made invaluable contributions in the development of this resource. A special "thank you" to the following reviewers: James Williams, Human Resources Training Consultant, Riverdale, NY, and Beverly A. Brown, CEO/Principal Associate WorkSmarts: Staff Development Services, Brooklyn, NY, and also to my continuously supportive editor, Andrea Edwards of Triple SSS Press Media Development, and Project Manager, Dr. Inell Bolls of Thomson/South-Western. I also acknowledge the generous support of my husband, Glenn, and my son, Brant, who provided unending support and encouragement during the writing of this book.

MAKING CONNECTIONS

Working together we can achieve extraordinary results.

©ROSE ALCORN

A Company Profile:
Connecting for Quality Care

Cultural diversity is both a fact of life and a source of innovation at a large home health-care agency operating in New York. Because its patient population represents many different countries, languages, and ethnicities, the agency has found that its ability to consistently achieve service excellence is directly tied to its diverse professional population.

Each professional strives to meet the ongoing challenges inherent in providing superior care in an even more diverse, regulated, and competitive environment. Field staff witness changing demographics and are, as a result, continually supported in the development of intercultural skills. Such support is provided because organizational leaders know that sensitivity to cultural difference is often the key to creating and maintaining positive connections with patients in an increasingly diverse community.

As a demonstration of the agency's commitment to diversity, several multicultural programs have successfully been established. These programs are driven by the awareness that patients often feel more comfortable and, in some cases, recover more quickly when they receive care from nurses and other caregivers who speak their language and reflect their cultural and ethnic backgrounds.[1] The multicultural programs provide a large pool of healthcare workers and translators who not only speak foreign languages, but can understand and accommodate the cultural needs, values, and customs of many different ethnic groups. Services for the non-native patient are many: multilingual hotlines and educational materials, nutritional plans tailored for various ethnic groups, family-centered care, and partnerships with various ethnic organizations.

This agency's multicultural approach has resulted in a mutually beneficial arrangement because it has managed to rapidly expand its reach—making services available to new populations—while building and maintaining an increasingly successful track record in quality care.

GOALS:

Upon completion of this Workshop, the reader will:

➤ Understand changing national demographics and the concept of a "global workforce"

➤ Understand the implications and associated benefits of cultural diversity

➤ Develop an awareness of the personal, professional, and organizational costs of low intercultural competence

➤ Appreciate the importance of organizational culture in the achievement of success

➤ Recognize ways to move beyond awareness and meet the challenges presented by diversity

Intercultural Competence Pre-Assessment

Please complete the following pre-assessment to identify your current level of intercultural competence. Read each statement below and note the extent to which you agree or disagree with it, where 1 = not at all, 2 = somewhat, and 3 = very much so.

_____ 1. I am aware of demographic changes taking place in America and understand the implications for me, my community, and the workplace.

_____ 2. I am aware of the challenges and associated benefits of cultural diversity.

_____ 3. I am always aware of the stereotypes that shape my interactions with others.

_____ 4. I don't draw negative conclusions when others do or see things differently.

_____ 5. I know what culture is and how it influences my particular values and the unique way in which I view and interpret the world.

_____ 6. I have spent time exploring the many facets of my culture and how it differs from others.

_____ 7. I recognize that although someone may look very different from me, it is possible that we share a lot in common.

_____ 8. I am aware that because cultures are complex and multifaceted, I can never assume anything about others.

_____ 9. I always strive to get beyond obvious differences such as ethnicity, race, and gender so that I might build effective intercultural relationships.

_____ 10. I make it a point to learn about other cultures.

_____ 11. When I meet someone from another ethnic group or country, I demonstrate an interest in understanding his/her culture.

_____ 12. I understand my role in facilitating effective intercultural interactions.

_____ 13. I am confident in my abilities to recognize and resolve intercultural conflict.

_____ 14. I recognize that building the skills necessary to engage in intercultural relationships is an ongoing process.

If you indicated "somewhat" or "not at all" to any of the above statements, then you will benefit from the exercises and information provided in this workbook. They will guide you toward greater self-awareness, confidence, and competence in building effective intercultural communication and relationship skills.

THE EVER-CHANGING FACE OF AMERICA

> " There was never a core America in which everyone looked the same, spoke the same language, worshipped the same gods, and believed the same things. "
> —Robert Hughes

Celebrate common ground, even as you celebrate diversity.

©RYAN MCVAY/PHOTODISC/GETTY IMAGES

Pick up any history book and you'll quickly be reminded that America was built on a foundation of diverse cultural contributions. Unique in this regard, America has drawn and continues to draw diverse groups to its shores. Each wave of immigration may have brought with it different faces, customs, and languages, but the result is nonetheless the same: America remains an increasingly multicultural society.

Cultural diversity is a multifaceted issue—one that addresses difference along any of a number of well-known cultural dimensions such as age, educational level, economic class, ethnicity, gender, race, and sexual orientation. Additional nuances come from less obvious cultural dimensions including personality type, career field, where you grew up, or even where you live. Adopting an effective approach to intercultural relationship building requires an understanding of the varying dimensions of cultural difference along with a broader understanding of global shifts and their impact on national workforce dynamics.

One such shift is the change in attitude among more recent immigrants. While the "melting pot" analogy represents a long-standing American expectation that newly arrived immigrants will assimilate into the dominant American culture, a Society for Human Resource Management report identified "an increasingly outspoken loyalty to cultural heritage among ethnic minorities," which they reported is also serving to intensify the impact of diversity in the workplace.[2]

The trend toward separation, rather than assimilation, presents new challenges for businesses striving to build strong organizational cultures that effectively optimize the contributions of an increasingly diverse workforce. A proactive approach involves studying international trends, which can provide valuable information that organizations can then use to determine the most effective strategies for responding to change.

In order to understand how global shifts are influencing American workforce demographics, it is helpful to review the most recent census reports.

Acculturation

the process of adjusting and adapting to a new and different culture[3]

According to Chaney and Martin, acculturation has four dimensions[4]:

➤ *Integration:* The individuals become a part of the new culture while maintaining their own culture.

➤ *Separation:* The individuals maintain their own culture and resist the new culture.

➤ *Assimilation:* The individuals are absorbed into the new culture and give up the old culture.

➤ *Deculturation:* The individuals forfeit their original culture but do not accept the new culture, resulting in confusion and anxiety.

CENSUS 2000 SAYS

What's happening abroad? Based on U.S. Census Bureau 2000 reports, all evidence points to the inescapable reality that just as the market for products and services has extended across national, cultural, and ethnic boundaries in the United States and abroad, so too has the labor market. Workforce growth in all advanced nations has been slowing down, while growth in developing nations continues to increase. As a result, workforce projections paint an increasingly clear picture of an international labor market where advanced nations such as the United States will compete with other advanced nations to attract the international market's most skilled workers.

> "The United States will find itself in competition against other developed nations to lure the world's best and brightest workers and in competition against less developed nations to keep America's best employers and jobs."
>
> —Hudson Institute

What's happening here at home? All signs point to an increasingly diverse domestic workplace. According to Census 2000, women, minorities, and immigrants account for most of the current growth in the U.S. labor force. The workforce is also aging; the Bureau of Labor Statistics indicates that workers aged 45 to 64 represent the fastest growing segment. Demand for skilled, educated workers continues to increase, while the number of American high school and college graduates is decreasing. Add to these key points the declining birthrates among majority groups, and the result is an impending shortage in traditional domestic workforce labor. Figure 1.1 from the Census 2000 statistics further highlights this shift.

CHANGE, CHANGE, CHANGE

Combined, these trends provide us with a compelling picture of the not-too-distant future. In fact, they indicate changes that have already been set in motion:

Census 2000 Statistics[5]:

For Americans 70 and older, there are 5.63 (non-Hispanic) Whites for every non-White.

For those under the age of 40, there are 1.72 (non-Hispanic) Whites for every non-White.

For those under the age of 10, there are 1.47 (non-Hispanic) Whites for every non-White.

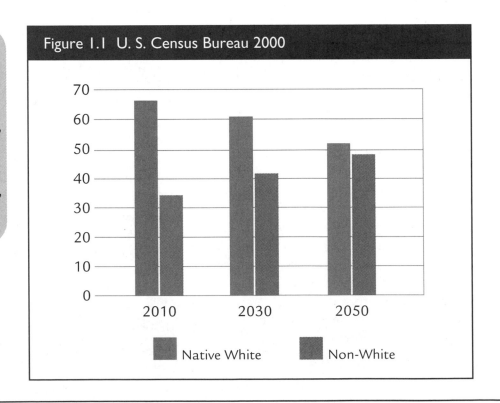

Figure 1.1 U. S. Census Bureau 2000

Native White   Non-White

- The American labor force will shrink and age, while the workforce in developing nations will grow and offer younger workers.

- Organizations will increasingly look toward an international labor market for skilled, educated labor to maintain high productivity and innovation levels.

- American businesses will increasingly be comprised of a skilled workforce that is not traditional or native White male.

We can already see evidence that companies are adopting new strategies to position themselves for success in this increasingly global market, since many have begun studying market trends and aligning communications with the interests, needs, and values of diverse audiences. Just tune into a foreign language television station and you will see familiar American products being marketed in new and unique ways.

There are implications for the American employee as well. Ashkanasy, Hartel, and Daus observed that given the trend toward a service economy, organizations will need to understand how to effectively serve and retain a customer base that is now significantly more diverse.[6] Given the trend toward knowledge work, organizational viability will ultimately depend on the knowledge, skills, abilities, and attitudes of employees. These observations translate into the following:

- Competence in emotional intelligence and intercultural communication have become critical.

- Management practices that encourage innovation, a learning culture, and competency in working across cultural difference have become essential.

- Leaders, managers, and employees who learn to develop the awareness and skills to most effectively thrive in a diverse environment will ultimately be the most competitive, and therefore, the most successful.

INTERCULTURAL COMPETENCE: A NEW CRITICAL SKILL

Intercultural competence is now a critical requirement, and as such, suggests that organizations develop new proactive strategies that will enable them to compete in a global market, while individuals seek to develop the skills that will prepare them to interact with and work alongside individuals from different cultural backgrounds and perspectives. As competencies are made up of an essential combination of knowledge, skills, and attitude, intercultural competence addresses:

- *Knowledge:* Developing a keen awareness regarding the importance of culture, specifically one's own culture, in building effective intercultural relationships

- *Skills:* Building constructive communication and conflict resolution skills for more effective intercultural experiences

- *Attitude:* Understanding the benefits associated with cultural diversity, and therefore, the importance of building effective intercultural skills

Quick Culture Facts

- Latino Americans come from a variety of cultural and racial backgrounds.

- Asian-Indians represent the most rapidly growing segment within the Asian-American population.[7]

- Not all "Black" individuals in this country are African-American; some are Caribbean, others have migrated from Africa, and still others consider themselves biracial or multiracial.

- Almost half of all immigrants entering the United States arrived in just the last 12 years.[8]

- Women are the primary investors in more than half of U.S. households.[9]

Online Research— Diverse Origins of Everyday Things

Can you imagine an everyday existence without the influence of diverse cultural groups? For example, did you know that

➤ Coffee comes from Ethiopia and dates back to A.D. 600.

TIP:

Entering "invention" + the specific item you wish to research may yield more results that are directly relevant.

➤ Researchers found that the toothbrush, a centuries-old instrument that dates back to 15th-century China, is more valued than cars, computers, cell phones, or microwave ovens, according to a recent survey[10].

➤ Garrett Augustus Morgan, an African-American, patented an early traffic signal in 1923 that greatly improved safety on America's streets and roadways and was the basis for modern traffic signal systems.

➤ It was a woman, Mary Anderson, who invented the windshield wiper in 1903.

Online Research

Identify five to ten items you use in your everyday life and run a quick online search to explore the various cultural influences they represent.

BENEFITS AND IMPLICATIONS OF CULTURAL DIVERSITY

Evidence for the many benefits of cultural diversity has been consistently documented over the years. A brief summary of two research studies on the effects of diversity on group performance follows:

➤ 1961: Mixed-gender groups produced higher quality solutions more consistently than did male-only groups. No male-only group ever scored higher than a mixed-gender group.[11]

➤ 1992: Ethnically and racially diverse groups outperformed Anglo-only groups in the generation of new ideas that were judged to be effective and feasible.[12]

Further evidence indicating that we must consider cultural diversity as a direct link to organizational success comes from a 2001 survey of human resource professionals conducted by the Society for Human Resource Management (SHRM) and *Fortune* magazine, which found the following[13]:

➤ 83 percent of respondents believe cultural diversity improves corporate culture.

➤ 79 percent believe it improves employee morale.

➤ 76 percent believe it results in greater retention.

➤ 75 percent believe it facilitates recruitment of the best and the brightest.

➤ 68 percent believe it decreases complaints and litigation.

➤ 59 percent believe it enhances productivity, team effectiveness, and innovation.

"... Ninety-two percent of respondents [in a SHRM/*Fortune* magazine study of workplace diversity initiatives] said their organization's diversity management program had improved the bottom line.

—Society for Human Resource Management

Other findings have addressed the role of cultural diversity in helping organizations to maintain a competitive edge by:

➤ Improving the quality of the organization's workforce

➤ Leading to greater creativity, employee engagement, commitment, and motivation

➤ Providing greater access to and an ability to effectively meet the needs of new diverse markets

➤ Facilitating greater adaptability to changing market needs

Enabling the contributions of diverse groups results in a stronger organizational culture, higher quality solutions, and increased innovation—key requirements for competitive advantage in today's economy where "faster, better, cheaper," and most recently, "personalized," are the rules. Organizations and employees must therefore:

➤ Be open to exploring and learning about the effects of diversity.

➤ Adopt a broader, more strategic view of diversity, rather than view it as a mere compliance measure.

➤ Support employees in the development of key skills required to facilitate constructive dialogue and conflict resolution.

➤ Be ready and willing to adapt to changing market conditions—"the major business challenge of the 21st century."

➤ Commit to inclusion and acceptance of cultural diversity as a long-term strategy.

The above requirements translate into specific leadership competencies:

➤ Ability to develop intercultural communication, conflict resolution, and coaching skills

➤ Intelligent management of diverse teams

➤ Ability and willingness to support different work styles

➤ Ability to encourage and enable all employees to apply their unique talents and skills for the benefit of the team/business

➤ Ability to hire qualified talent who reflect the diversity in the local, national, and/or global market

➤ Ability to motivate and engage all employees to ensure maximum productivity and innovation

> " Deliberately positioning human differences throughout the organization is one way of gaining non-quantifiable advantages such as innovativeness and effectiveness. "
> —Cornelius Grove

CASE STUDIES

1. American Express has successfully built an environment in which managers and executives are encouraged to and held accountable for integrating diversity into their business objectives. **Result:** The number of senior women at American Express in the United States, which includes women of color, increased from 19 percent in 1990 to 31 percent in 2000.[14]

2. The University of North Carolina Health Care System identified an opportunity to better meet the needs of its growing Hispanic employee and patient population. First, the team committed to translating all written orientation materials into Spanish and ensuring that qualified interpreters would be present during new employee orientations. Second, the team decided to offer English as a Second Language classes and Spanish language classes to all employees. **Result:** The number of new Hispanic patients doubled from 3,000 in 1995 to 6,000 in 1999.[15]

> "Attracting women and 'minorities' will become less an issue of fairness, though it will remain so, of course, and more a strategy to maintain a high-skill, high-knowledge workforce. Properly construed, diversity policies are aimed at this goal already.

—Hudson Institute

Cultural diversity doesn't just benefit organizations; employees also benefit from an enriched life experience, increased creativity, greater workplace innovations, expanded personal networks, and improved communication skills.

Expand your personal network.

Interactive Group Activity: Finding Value in Cultural Difference

Part A

Identify three to five cultural labels to describe yourself (e.g., male/female, Irish/American, Black/White, Southerner/Northerner, white collar/blue collar). Review and answer the following questions for **each** label you identified.

➤ As a/an [cultural category], what three things do I most value?

➤ How has being a/an [cultural category] shaped the person that I am and how I see the world?

➤ What life lessons might I not have learned were it not for my experience as a/an [cultural category] in this society?

➤ What do I appreciate most about being a/an [cultural category]?

➤ What do I find most challenging about being a/an [cultural category]?

➤ What unique contributions do I feel [cultural category] offer in the workplace?

Part B

➤ Identify one person you know well who identifies with one or more cultural categories that do not apply to you. Explain the exercise to that person and ask his/her permission to engage in a discussion about culture and worldviews. Once the individual agrees, have him/her identify his/her own cultural labels and reflect on the same questions, providing his/her perspective on each.

➤ Alternatively, you can choose to research a different culture and explore the associated worldviews. There are many online resources and e-books that address the specific cultural characteristics of various ethnicities and nationalities.

TIP:
Be careful not to interrupt or challenge different perspectives or views; instead ask questions that will encourage the other individual to share more information with you about how he or she views the world.

MOVING BEYOND AWARENESS AND MEETING THE CHALLENGES

> " When HR practices support the creation of a workforce that has the skills needed to turn diversity into an advantage, diversity is more likely to lead to positive performance outcomes. "
>
> —Society for Human Resource Management

You may be wondering why, if cultural diversity is so beneficial to both organizations and employees, are some companies and individuals resistant to it? The energy behind this resistance usually stems from one of the following three issues: 1) resistance to or fear of *change*, 2) fear of all things *different*, and/or 3) resistance to *learning*.

Fear and resistance reflect attitudes, which are often difficult to influence. It takes an appropriate mix of education, skills training, and ongoing support to allay fears and to shift attitudes. Employees must understand how cultural diversity ties into organizational strategy, as well as the benefits of such strategies. They must be trained in key communication, conflict resolution, and intercultural skills. Organizational programs, practices, and initiatives must align with and provide support for these strategies. Perhaps of most importance, leaders must serve as role models, demonstrating the same behaviors that will help to shape an inclusive culture.

The truth is that cultural diversity initially does present difficult challenges, such as increased opportunities for misinterpretation, miscommunication, and therefore conflict. Employees know this. Organizational leaders know this. Current organizational realities provide additional challenges, especially for companies taking their first very important steps toward incorporating cultural diversity as a competitive strategy. For example, a Society for Human Resource Management (SHRM) Survey on Barriers to Advancement found that 74 percent of human resource professionals agree that minorities face barriers in the workplace and that these barriers stem from stereotypes, preconceptions based on race or ethnicity, exclusion from information networks, and lack of mentoring opportunities or role models. Statistics also show that women and minorities tend to be clustered in staff positions and in low-to-middle management levels, therefore, ensuring that the contributions from these segments of the workforce are solicited and utilized becomes a key initiative in the pursuit of an inclusive environment. A recent backlash from White males—they claim diversity initiatives, rather than promoting an equal playing field, only turn the tables and place White males at a disadvantage—has also challenged organizations to find new ways of involving and considering the contributions of this traditional group when determining strategies to shape culturally inclusive environments.

While these challenges may initially prove difficult to navigate, case studies have shown that ongoing education, training, communication, and support can help to ultimately transform the "us versus them" mentality, which tends to define many organizational cultures, into a more collaborative, or inclusive, mindset. Working effectively across cultural difference requires a concerted effort, an assumption of accountability by all employees, a long-term focus, and organization-wide development of greater cultural awareness and communication skills.

> " The ultimate goal of diversity training for employees, managers, and executives is the creation of a workplace 'culture of inclusion.' A culture of inclusion is one in which employees adjust flexibly to people with different characteristics and backgrounds, making it easier for the latter to develop productive, satisfying work relationships. "
>
> —Cornelius Grove

Remember that innovation and leadership have many faces.

COSTS OF LOW INTERCULTURAL COMPETENCE

Given changing demographics and the increasingly global scope of the labor market, the organization that fails to create an organizational culture that supports inclusiveness will likely face:

➤ Low levels of employee attraction and retention—nontraditional employees who feel pressured to conform and abandon their unique strengths will move to other organizations that will accept them on their own terms

➤ Threat to their ability to compete in an increasingly global market, and therefore, their ability to survive long term

➤ A higher rate of lawsuits

The number of job discrimination complaints filed with the Equal Employment Opportunity Commission (EEOC) increased by 4 percent in 2002—the highest in seven years. The highest growth in this post-9/11 era was represented by religious discrimination (21%), age discrimination (14.5%), and national origin bias (13%).[16] A broader perspective demonstrates the significant impact on our nation's resources when you consider that these lawsuits make up about a quarter of the federal civil docket.[17]

The implications for individuals are equally as significant. Effectively marketing oneself in a highly diverse labor market where building effective working relationships with international colleagues will increasingly become a requirement will rely in large part on the ability to demonstrate a high level of intercultural competence. Those who choose not to develop these critical skills will face greater challenges in competing against skilled international talent, thriving in the workplace, developing their careers, and pursuing opportunities to join successful organizations. Fortunately, the first step to developing intercultural competence is relatively safe because it involves self-exploration. Workshop 2 will guide you through a more in-depth discussion of culture and analysis of the components that shape your particular cultural lens.

> " Common sense suggests and research confirms that to produce superior performance within heterogeneous groups, members need to have advance awareness of the ways in which they are different from and similar to the other members and how this may impact their work.
>
> —H.C. Triandis "

Online Research—Using Keywords

For additional resources and information on making intercultural connections, use the following keywords to search online: cultural diversity, diversity, intercultural communication, and managing diversity.

Some organizations working to foster effective intercultural relationships in schools and/or the workplace are the Society for Human Resource Management, Diversity Inc., IMDiversity, BiasHelp, Conflict Resolution Education Network, and the Southern Poverty Law Center: Teaching Tolerance Project.

Points to Remember

➤ National and international demographics are changing, introducing the concept of a "global workforce."

➤ Benefits of cultural diversity include optimized team effectiveness, productivity, and business innovation.

➤ Intercultural competence will better enable Americans to thrive professionally and personally; low intercultural competence will result in decreased competitiveness, professional effectiveness, and career opportunity.

➤ Organizational culture will play a large role in an organization's ability to effectively compete and ultimately survive in an international labor market.

➤ Awareness is only the first step. We must be willing to develop the skills required to relate interpersonally across many different kinds of cultural boundaries.

> " If we as individuals and organizations are to thrive in a world of plural cultures, we must learn not only to respect differences but to enjoy them, not only to familiarize ourselves with different cultural traditions, but to take advantage of the enrichment gained through our interactions with the members of those cultures. To do this we must recognize our own roots within our own culture, our own basis of understanding and the values that tend to influence us.
>
> —Society for Human Resource Management "

Endnotes

1. The Visiting Nurse Service of New York Agency Web site, http://www.vnsny.org

2. Jana Howard Carey & Larry R. Seegull, "Beware the Native Tongue: National Origin and English-Only Rules," *Society for Human Resource Management Legal Report,* 1995

3. H.P. Hazuda, M.P. Stern, & S.M. Hoffner, "Acculturation and assimilation among Mexican Americans: Sales and population-based data," *Social Science Quarterly*, Vol. 69, 1988

4. L.H. Chaney & J.S. Martin, *Intercultural Business Communication*, Prentice Hall, 1995, 2000

5. Diversity Inc., *The Business Case for Diversity*, Fourth Edition, Allegiant Media, 2003

6. N.M. Ashkanasy, C.E.J. Härtel, & C.S. Daus, "Diversity and Emotion: The New Frontiers in Organizational Behavior Research," *Journal of Management*, Vol. 28, No. 3, 2002

7. Diversity Inc., op.cit.

8. Diversity Inc., op.cit.

9. Society for Human Resource Management, "Workplace Diversity," SHRM Diversity Initiative White Paper, 1999

10. Peggy Noonan, "Best Invention Ever: Your Toothbrush," USA Weekend Magazine, Science Special Report, June 8, 2003

11. L. Hoffman & N. Maier, "Quality and Acceptance of Problem Solutions by Members of Homogeneous and Heterogeneous Groups," *Journal of Abnormal and Social Psychology*, Vol. 62, 1961

12. Cornelius Grove & Associates, "Diversity in Business," SHRM White Paper, 1995, Reviewed November 2002 by the Society for Human Resource Management

13. Society for Human Resource Management, "Census 2000 Toolkit"

14. Cornelius Grove & Associates, op.cit.

15. Cornelius Grove & Associates, op.cit.

16. Diversity Inc., op.cit.

17. Society for Human Resource Management, "Census 2000 Toolkit"

DECONSTRUCTING CULTURE

Who you really are becomes clear only once you examine the various components that have shaped your unique cultural lens.

Profile of a Multicultural Individual

My mother was born into a cross-racial family; her mother was Irish, born in the deep South, and her father was the son of an African slave and a strict Christian Cherokee woman. Color, culture, and religion played significant roles in her upbringing, shaping many of her views on life. From her, I learned that skin color does not matter unless we make it so, that what makes a person good or bad is not based on what is on the outside, but rather what is on the inside, and that a passive approach to conflict is sometimes best.

Grandma was a fiery redhead with freckles that covered her skin. A strong southern woman, she left Virginia because her pastor refused to marry her and my grandfather. "They'll burn down my church if I marry you," the pastor said, and so she moved to New York City. From her, I learned that women could be strong, independent, and still be nurturing, that I should always speak my authentic voice and not rely on others to find my own truths, and that intelligence is not bound to any particular age, gender, or race.

Papi (the Latino reference for "father") was born and raised in Puerto Rico. His background constitutes a racial and ethnic blend of Spanish-European, Caribbean-African, and Taino Native American. When he moved to the United States, he experienced culture shock as a result of the racial division he encountered. Here, the outdated but predominant lingering shadow of the "one drop rule" means he is expected to categorize himself as Black or African-American. In response to this limited American perspective, he makes the effort to educate others on *Boricua* culture—the ethnic and racial harmony represented by Puerto Rican culture. From him, I learned that culture is not always visible, but nonetheless, more important than skin color, that being a woman meant that I had better learn to cook well and be a good host, and that having a sense of humor in life is helpful.

These individuals have had the most influence in my life. That my ancestors had been marrying across color and culture lines for over three generations meant that I spent most of my life crossing back and forth across cultural lines, speaking different languages and integrating different values, beliefs, and perspectives into the whole of my self-identity. Contrary to prevailing stereotypes of the multicultural individual, I believe this has been a valuable exercise.

Negative stereotypes of the "confused" biracial or multiracial individual are reflected in terms such as "tragic mulatto" or "mixed-up." It is my belief that these terms reflect, instead, the confusion most Americans feel about race and culture. Ironically, most Americans are blind to the influence of culture in their own lives, failing to understand how their culture truly differs from or compares to others. While this understanding is key to intercultural effectiveness, researchers confirm that this inability tends, unfortunately, to be a predominant American cultural trait.

Upon completion of this Workshop, the reader will:

➤ Identify his/her response to culture difference and define culture shock

➤ Identify the components (the three P's) of culture

➤ Begin to understand how cultures differ

➤ Deconstruct American culture and his/her own unique culture

RESPONDING TO CULTURE DIFFERENCE

What's your general response to culture difference? Do you tend to approach it with curiosity, avoid it at all costs, or respond as if it doesn't exist? At one time in our history, we believed that the solution to equality and intercultural harmony was color-blindness, or perhaps more broadly, blindness to any cultural difference. This philosophy still lingers so that from time to time, someone approaches me and proudly proclaims to be color-blind.

Being color-blind means you cannot see color. Blindness to difference means you cannot see that which is different. Hiding our heads in the sand and pretending that we do not see what is different means we err in making the assumption that we are the same—that those who are different think as we do, believe as we do, and share the same practices and social norms. The **ethnocentrism**—the tendency to evaluate other groups according to the values and standards of one's own cultural group, particularly with the conviction that one's own culture is superior to others—inherent in failing to acknowledge what is different does not help us to build the skills we need to effectively navigate cultural difference. Quite the contrary, it has the potential to result in greater conflict as it often renders the "other" invisible or invalid.

The benefits of seeing difference are clearly visible when we explore companies with multicultural marketing practices. These companies reap benefits such as increased revenues and better relationships with new customers, as they are able to effectively expand into new markets and deliver services and products tailored to meet the needs and interests of an increasingly diverse market. We must understand then that the goal is not to achieve color-blindness, but rather a curiosity about and appreciation for the mutual value that can result from acknowledging culture difference.

> " Greetings! I am pleased to see that we are different. May we together become greater than the sum of both of us. "
>
> —Vulcan Greeting (*Star Trek*)

Culture shock—the disorientation and frustration we experience when we encounter different cultural rules and norms—is a typical reaction to culture difference. Because our own cultures are often invisible to us, taken for granted, emotionally charged and/or taught to represent moral high ground, we have a tendency to assume that something is wrong with others, not with us, and to define our own culture as "more natural," "more rational," or "more civilized." In doing so, we undervalue the other culture by defining it as "immoral," "irrational," or "uncivilized."

As this same orientation tends to be assumed by the other culture as well, the result often becomes a cross-cultural impasse, which further fuels the initial culture shock. Moving beyond this paralyzing response requires a willingness to acknowledge the legitimacy and relevance of other people's way of life within their cultural contexts.

Culture shock is a natural response to culture difference.

 ©PHOTODISC COLLECTION/GETTY IMAGES

The National Foreign Language Standards define the **three P's of culture** as the philosophical perspectives, behavioral practices, and products—both intangible and tangible—of a society.[2]

➤ **Perspectives** include beliefs, thought processes, values, and **worldviews** (our mental models or ideas about the way the world works)—encompassing the "philosophies" of a culture.

➤ **Practices** include social norms, approaches to communication and conflict, orientation to hierarchy, power, class, status, and gender roles—constituting the "norms" of a culture.

➤ **Products** represent tangibles such as food, clothing, books, and tools, and intangibles such as songs, parables, dances, rituals, language, and laws—comprising the "artifacts" of a culture.

There are two important things to remember about culture. The first is that culture is ever changing. The three P's continuously interact with one another in complex ways. Since historical as well as current environmental realities play a significant role in shaping culture, each dimension tends to evolve over time. Collectively, a given culture's perspectives, practices, and products play a significant role in defining the unique expectations, assumptions, humor, and symbols of a culture. Therefore, it is common to observe great differences from one generation to the next. For example, do you remember the beehive, Afro, or mullet? How about the different comedies that made Americans laugh over the years, such as the *Three Stooges, Barney Miller,* the *Brady Bunch,* or the *Odd Couple*? It is very likely that a young person today would find the unique brand of fashion sense, humor, or ideals from bygone eras somewhat different from those enjoyed today.

The second thing to remember about culture is that a broad description of a group (e.g., all Americans) seldom serves

Ironically, every time we encounter someone who differs from us in thought, manner, practice, or appearance, we have a perfect opportunity to learn something about ourselves, about how we uniquely view the world. If we first understand ourselves, we can then understand how we are truly alike or different from others.

SO, WHAT IS CULTURE ANYWAY?

Culture is a complex and multifaceted product of group life, a necessary means of creating structure and order, and is generally defined as "a learned system of meaning and behavior that is passed from one generation to the next[1]. Each group has its own particular cultural characteristics, so it is generally difficult for outsiders to understand or make sense of their cultural norms without first understanding the associated history and environmental context.

as an accurate description for each individual functioning within it, as each may also belong to various subgroups within the culture (e.g., African-Americans, Mexican-Americans, women, men, Amish). In addition, those subgroups can often be broken down into further subgroups (e.g., Black: Caribbean, African, Latin, biracial or multiracial).

Proverbs and Culture

Proverbs—pithy statements of wisdom—serve as a window into a particular culture's worldview. As you read those listed below, consider the perspectives these proverbs might reflect. Can you identify any others you might have come across throughout your upbringing? If so, what might they reflect about your culture?

African Proverbs[3]

➤ All lizards lie on their bellies, but nobody knows which of them suffers a stomach ache. (Nigeria)

➤ Nobody refers to part of his body as a hump. (Refers to relatives, Nigeria)

American Proverbs

➤ Every man for himself.

➤ Good fences make good neighbors.

Arab Proverbs

➤ The son of a son is dear. The son of a daughter a stranger.

➤ A big-mouth person's words and point of view are worthless. (Iran)

Asian Proverbs

➤ The nail that sticks up will be hammered down. (Japan)

➤ He who asks is a fool for five minutes, but he who does not ask remains a fool forever. (China)

European Proverbs

➤ Time is money.

➤ One father is better at caring for ten children than ten children are for one father.

Native American Proverbs

➤ A people without history is like wind on the buffalo grass. (Sioux)

➤ We will be known forever by the tracks we leave. (Dakota)

DIFFERENT STROKES, DIFFERENT FOLKS

Working together, the three P's create cultures that differ from others in several key ways. Some of the more salient differences include the following: orientation to groups, orientation to time, orientation to power and authority, orientation to gender roles, and value systems. A brief description of each is provided in the following sections.[4]

Orientation to Groups

Individualists speak for themselves, value independence, and emphasize individual achievements. Their workplaces may utilize individual reward and recognition programs or issue salary increases based on individual performance. Their motto might be "You have to take care of number one."

Collectivists allow the group to speak for the individual, place great value on group membership, extend decision-making beyond the nuclear family to the extended family, and emphasize teamwork and harmony. These cultures tend to make a point of collectively and wholeheartedly participating in team-building activities. Their motto might be "There is no I in TEAM."

Orientation to Time

Clock-oriented cultures are likely to focus on the here and now, emphasize doing rather than being, and adhere to schedules, punctuality, and organization around clocks. Time is viewed in a linear fashion. Daily planners, Palm Pilots, and digital calendars are familiar and essential products within these cultures.

Event-oriented cultures, on the other hand, emphasize completion of an event over a strict adherence to schedules. They prefer to fully finish one task before beginning another, regardless of the amount of time it takes, and tend to think of time in a somewhat more abstract manner, viewing it as cyclical rather than linear. It may be customary, for example, to spend ample time welcoming a visitor before rushing to the business at hand. Imagine the clock-oriented individual's reaction when he arrives in an event-oriented culture with a tight itinerary to find that meetings seldom start "on time."

Orientation to Power and Authority

Egalitarian cultures work hard to ensure opportunities for upward mobility and a voice for all. Equal opportunity programs may be established so that women and other members of less dominant social groups do not face obstacles within the workplace. In this context, for example, directly challenging the CEO might demonstrate initiative and win you that promotion.

Hierarchical cultures are comfortable with status difference and may prefer formal use of titles and degrees. In some cultures, you may be born to a particular station in life and have little chance of upward mobility. Directly challenging the CEO in this context, for example, might not be such a good idea and only end up costing you your job.

Orientation to Gender Roles

Male-dominated cultures may prohibit access to education, ownership, and professions by women, enabling men to make key decisions for women. For example, in some cultures, a common practice is for the husband to decide what medical care and services his wife will receive.

Egalitarian cultures enable women to function as proactive members of society —ensuring rights to property ownership, political participation, higher education, and career advancement—independent of any male influence.

Values

Cultural values capture varying perspectives regarding the importance of relationships between human beings and nature. Examples include a prevailing belief that "materialism is bad" or that cultural products should be made from natural ingredients instead of synthetic ones.

Cultural values also capture varying perspectives regarding social interactions and practices. Examples include the belief that "showing your elders respect is important" or that social practices such as "Sweet 16," "La Quinceanera" (a Mexican celebration of a young girl's coming of age), or "Bar/Bat Mitzvah" celebrations mark an important transition to adulthood.

> " Each of us confronts a material, a social and a spiritual universe that must be structured so that we can negotiate our way through the maze of life. "
> —K. Leung & M. H. Bond

Again, it is important to remember that not every individual within a given culture will reflect all of the characteristics associated with that group. Because cultures evolve, generational differences are commonly encountered. Individuals often belong to various cultural subgroups— defined by geographic region, education, or other dimensions—and their particular worldviews or behaviors may, at times, be indicative of these other cultural influences.

Cultural Assessment

Part A

Reflect on the ways in which cultures differ and write your thoughts regarding your own cultural orientation in the space provided below.

_____
_____
_____
_____
_____
_____
_____
_____

What values, beliefs, and experiences shape and define your unique worldview?

Part B

What might the advantages and disadvantages of your particular orientation be in a diverse workplace? In other words, how might you help or hinder a diverse team?

My orientation to time	Advantages	Disadvantages
My orientation to gender roles	Advantages	Disadvantages
My orientation to groups	Advantages	Disadvantages
My orientation to power and authority	Advantages	Disadvantages
My cultural values	Advantages	Disadvantages

DECONSTRUCTING AMERICAN CULTURE

It is impossible for one individual to study the characteristics and nuances of every culture in existence today, but understanding how cultures differ on a fundamental level, such as that presented by the three P's framework, is a valuable first step toward understanding other cultures as well as your own. Americans, perhaps as a result of our unique history as a "melting pot" society, tend to be less aware of our own culture than others are of theirs. In fact, it is quite common to hear trainees of all backgrounds say, "I don't have a culture; I'm just American." Ask someone from another country to describe Americans, however, and you'll quickly learn that although American culture may be somewhat invisible to us, others do associate specific characteristics with our culture.

How Others View American Culture

Perspectives

➤ You appreciate capitalism and fiercely defend the idea of democracy.

➤ You are not very superstitious.

➤ You value and expect unique self-expression and independence.

➤ You focus primarily on the "here and now," which means that you're not overly concerned with the distant past or the very distant future.

➤ You expect that individuals in other countries will speak English.

Practices

➤ What to study in school or whom to marry is not an extended-family decision.

➤ If you're a woman, you feel free to make your own personal decisions.

➤ You cringe and apologize profusely if you are late to a major event, dinner, or business meeting.

➤ You ask "How are you?" as a way to simply say hello. You're really not expecting a drawn-out response.

➤ You think intellectual debate is a healthy activity in which adults should engage.

Products

➤ You expect to eat hot dogs at a baseball game.

➤ There's at least one McDonald's and one Burger King within driving distance, and probably a Taco Bell, a Wendy's, and a Boston Market as well.

➤ You probably know who won *American Idol* last year and the year before that.

➤ You wouldn't know how to prepare a live chicken if it flew into the pot.

➤ Your dream is to own a large home and an expensive car.

For how many of these cultural characteristics did you nod your head and think "Yes, that's me"? Again, remember that cultural subgroups (e.g., women, non-Whites) might align with some, but not all characteristics of a broader culture. Where your cultural lens (a perspective or expectation stemming from the context of one's culture) differs, it is helpful to think about which specific cultural groups or subgroups might have influenced you otherwise (e.g., race, religion, gender, class).

⊞ Online Research— American Cultural Characteristics

Conduct an online search on American culture to identify additional characteristics. Then choose an ethnic group from your ancestral background and conduct a similar search to explore how the two cultures compare and contrast. Note your findings in the space below.

American Culture Characteristics:

Ethnic Culture Characteristics:

Similarities

Differences

How do you handle the differences?

DECONSTRUCTING YOUR CULTURE

Effectively deconstructing your own culture—your worldviews, values, practices and social norms—requires taking a closer look at the various cultural dimensions that shape your unique experiences within the broader culture. Following is a brief look at some of the more salient aspects of culture: race, ethnicity, gender, religion, and generation.

Exploration of these cultural dimensions must begin with a clear understanding that the very definitions of terms such as *race, ethnicity, gender,* and *class* reflect ideas that are grounded in a particular social perspective, rather than in biological reality.

Race
Race can be defined as a human population distinguished as a more or less distinct group by variations in physical characteristics. However, scientists have recently discovered the following: Only 2 percent of our genes are ultimately

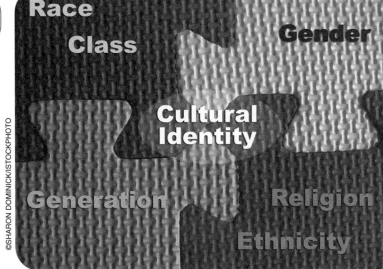

©SHARON DOMINICK/ISTOCKPHOTO

Cultural identity is like a puzzle; one lone piece can never provide a complete or an accurate picture of who you are.

responsible for the visible differences such as skin pigmentation or eyelid shape. Increasingly, scientists are coming to understand that the only meaningful racial category is that of human. Nonetheless, skin color carries with it significant historical, political, and social implications, and these are uniquely defined by each culture. How we are perceived and where we stand in relation to others on the social hierarchy stems biologically from a mere 2 percent of the gene pool and therefore, social interpretations vary crossculturally. For example, a person who is considered Black in one society might be considered non-Black in another. Individuals of mixed heritage in Brazil may consider themselves White and very well experience culture shock when they find that in the United States, they are considered Black. Despite scientific and crosscultural ambiguities, race remains a highly significant **social construct**, a system of beliefs—positive or negative—created by society to categorize and classify individuals.

Understanding the unique cultural beliefs we have inherited about race, culture, and culture difference, and exploring what we've learned about social hierarchies (specifically, our place in relation to others) requires an examination of our history; the messages we received from family members, friends, and other influences about these issues; and our own life experiences as they pertain to skin color.

> " The first step in the process is to look at yourself. While no one is born a bigot, by the time we are adults most of us have developed some prejudices. "
>
> —C. Stein-Larosa & E. Hofheimer Bettmann

A Note on White Privilege

While many American non-Whites are somewhat accustomed to thinking about what race means for them (it's hard not to, when society constantly reminds you that you are "other"), White Americans are less accustomed to such examination. Dr. Janet Helms, a researcher, professor, and author on the subject of White racial identity said, ". . . development of a positive, psychologically healthy White racial identity *requires* a decision to abandon racism. The first step toward abandonment of racism requires recognition of it".[5] Additionally, White racial identity development requires recognition of the general social privileges afforded Whites as a result of their position at the top of the social hierarchy.

A source of confusion for Whites on the issue of White privilege pertains to the undeniable reality that not all Whites have experienced easy lives, financial gains, or other tangible results generally assumed to be associated with "privilege." Kimberley Hohmann, author on race relations[6], offers the following examples to clarify the meaning of White privilege:

➤ Being able to turn on the television and see people of your race widely represented

➤ Never being asked to speak on behalf of your entire race

➤ Being able to buy "flesh" colored band-aids that closely match your skin color

➤ Being able to succeed without being called a credit to your race

➤ Being able to have a bad day without wondering what your race had to do with specific negative incidents

Although it is challenging, identifying and acknowledging the benefits associated with being White in America is a critical requirement for developing the ability to empathize, understand, and build effective crosscultural relationships.

How has race influenced your cultural lens?

Ethnicity

Race and ethnicity are often used interchangeably, although such use is incorrect. **Ethnicity** differs from race in that it represents social groups with a shared history, sense of identity, geography, and cultural roots, which may occur despite racial difference. For example, Puerto Ricans, who on the whole represent a blend of White, Red, and Black races, refer to themselves collectively as *Boricuas*, thereby embracing the racial blend that is characteristic of so many from this Latin ethnic group.

As a result of widespread improper use of the terms *race* and *ethnicity*, many Americans mistakenly believe that unless they are people of color, the term *ethnicity* does not apply to them. All of us, however, have one or more ethnic backgrounds, and therefore, cultural influences.

The important thing to remember about ethnicity is that ethnic groups have a shared identity and that these groups alone decide who does and does not belong. For example, many individuals who may be somewhat removed from their Native American ancestors later seek to rejoin the relevant tribal nation. They are often surprised to discover that community involvement and ability to relate to that nation's unique cultural practices and perspectives is, by many Native American communities, considered more important than the particular percentage of Native blood the individual has. In this context, many Native American communities are trying to protect against further erosion of long-standing tribal customs and norms; they alone decide who is and who is not a member of their group.

Understanding the perspectives and practices you have inherited from your ethnic background(s) also requires an examination of your history and the messages you received from family members about what is valued and what constitutes tradition in your particular culture.

How has your ethnic background influenced your cultural lens?

Gender

Gender, the condition of psychologically identifying as male or female, may be genetically linked in most cases.

Nonetheless, the expectations and social norms associated with each may differ significantly from one culture to the next. Gender differences are often observed, for example, in communication style and in the approach taken to building relationships.

Reflecting on the messages you received over the years about gender—your place in society and the role you inherited as a result—can provide valuable information about the cultural influences that have helped to shape your worldview. Similar to the concept of White privilege, American males must also be willing to recognize the power and status afforded them by society and recognize the effects that such power has on women.

How has gender influenced your cultural lens?

Religion

Religion plays a key role in shaping one's cultural lens, particularly in relation to the values adopted by a social group. Whether you currently practice a particular religion or not, understanding the religious influences in your family history can provide helpful information about the particular messages that may have been handed down and currently shape your worldview.

How has religion influenced your cultural lens?

Generation

In order to identify the influence of generation on our worldviews, we need only compare the ideals, social practices, etiquette rules, and cultural products with those of our grandparents, parents, and/or children. Watching movies or TV programs and reviewing commercials from an earlier period can also provide insight into generational cultural differences.

How has the generation in which you were born influenced your cultural lens?

Each of these cultural dimensions alone plays a powerful role in shaping your worldview. Combined, they provide a unique prescription for the cultural lens through which you alone view and interpret the world. Consider also that there are many other cultural dimensions that ultimately shape how you see, interpret, and interact with the world (e.g., class, education, profession). Once you have a greater understanding of your cultural lens and why you see things the way you do, you will then be better able to recognize the variety and complexity of influences that also serve to shape the perspectives of others.

Interactive Group Activity: Deconstructing Your Culture

Part A

For each cultural dimension described above (race, ethnicity, gender, religion, generation), reflect on your upbringing, life experiences, and your findings from Activity 2.2 to identify two or three key ways that each has shaped the three P's (perspectives, practices, and products) of your culture.

Part B

Working in groups, take turns sharing your findings with others. Listen for commonalities and differences and ask open-ended questions to clarify and/or solicit additional information.

Part A

	Perspectives	Practices	Products
Race			
Ethnicity			
Gender			
Religion			
Generation			

Part B

What were the similarities and differences?

_____
_____
_____
_____
_____

What was your reaction to culture difference?

_____
_____
_____
_____
_____

MOVING FORWARD

Deconstructing our cultural personalities is a challenging, but highly valuable exercise for both our personal and professional development. It is also one that requires ongoing self-awareness and an effort to consistently make visible that which is often invisible throughout our day-to-day interactions with others. Developing an awareness of our unique culture and its worldviews can help us to understand and influence how others perceive us and determine how effectively we interact with others.

Fortunately, every time we encounter difference, we also encounter an opportunity to learn something new about ourselves. If you travel to a foreign country and experience different customs, if you wonder why people from a particular country don't smile very much, or if someone reacts in an unexpected manner to something you say, remember to shift your focus from figuring out what is wrong with them and instead, know that your culture is showing.

Activity 2.4

Online Research—Using Keywords

Additional resources and information on culture can be accessed with the following online search terms: American culture, cross-culture communication, cultural diversity, ethnicity and culture, gender and culture, intercultural communication, proverbs, race and culture, and religion and culture.

Some specific resources for cross cultural studies include the *Journal of Cross-Cultural Psychology, Cultural Dynamics, Cultural Studies, Culture & Psychology,* and *Journal of Business Communication.*

Points to Remember

➤ *Culture shock* is a term for the disorientation and frustration we experience when we encounter different cultural rules and norms.

➤ Culture is a learned system of meaning and behavior, passed from one generation to the next. Culture is defined by the three P's—perspectives, practices, and products. Culture is ever changing and can be specific to subgroups (racial, ethnic, generational, religious, gender) within a broader culture.

➤ Some of the more salient ways in which cultures differ include orientation to

groups, orientation to time, orientation to power and authority, orientation to gender roles, and cultural values.

➤ There is an American culture, although it may be invisible to us as members, and it does differ, sometimes significantly, from that of other countries. Effectively deconstructing your own culture requires taking a closer look at the messages you have inherited and experiences you have had as a result of your race, ethnicity, gender, religion, and generation.

Endnotes

1. R. Carter & A. Qureshi, "A typology of philosophical assumptions in multicultural counseling and training." In J.G. Ponterroto, J.M. Casas, L.A. Suzuki, & C.M. Alexander, eds., *Handbook of Multicultural Counseling*, Sage, 1995

2. Genelle G. Morain, "Diversity Dissected; Human Commonalities and Cultural Differences," Founders Day Lecture, The University of Georgia Chapel, January 27, 2004

3. R. Pachocinski, *Proverbs of Africa: Human Nature in the Nigerian Oral Tradition*, Professors World Peace Academy, March 1997

4. Adapted in part from C.K. Tomoeda & K.A. Bayles, "Cultivating Cultural Competence in the Workplace, Classroom, and Clinic," *The ASHA Leader Online*, Feature Article, American Speech-Language-Hearing Association

5. J. E. Helms, Ph.D., *A Race Is a Nice Thing to Have: A Guide to Being a White Person or Understanding the White Persons in Your Life*, Content Communications, 1992

6. Kimberley Hohmann, About.com, Topic: Race Relations; White Privilege

LEARNING ABOUT MENTAL MODELS

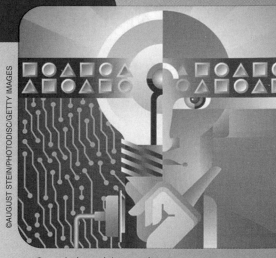

Our minds work in complex ways.

The Power of Mental Models

Jane Smith* grew up in a small town in Nebraska. After having earned her bachelor's degree in marketing, she decided to pursue job opportunities in a number of different cities. She had second thoughts about big city living, but she quickly landed a great job offer at a Fortune 500 company based in New York and decided to pursue it. The big city culture and degree of diversity she encountered, however, were a source of great culture shock.

In particular, Jane found the direct, often confrontational style of her coworkers, especially those from other ethnic groups, to be disconcerting. Although her job required her to establish positive working relationships with colleagues internally across a number of different functions, as well as externally with key clients, she considered them "strange people with strange ways." As a result, she was unsuccessful in achieving one of her key goals—networking to build effective relationships. Her ineffectiveness quickly became apparent to others, including her boss, who addressed it on several occasions.

Uncomfortable in her new surroundings, Jane began calling home every night to speak with old friends and family. They would plead with her to return home when they heard how unhappy she was. "We didn't think it was a good idea in the first place," they would say over and over again, so Jane began to seriously consider returning home.

Barely a year into her new role, however, Jane was suddenly laid off. Although the company stated it was for financial reasons, she suspected it had more to do with her not "fitting in" and not having formed close working relationships with a number of key colleagues.

Jane decided the time had come to return home. Unsure what this meant for her career, she turned her thoughts to the possibility of settling down and having children instead.

When she got home, Jane told everyone how right they had been in thinking that New York was not a good city in which to live. She was grateful to just be home, so she quickly accepted a job offer from her uncle to help out in the family store. After all, she thought, she could always use her marketing knowledge to help the store.

Jane Smith is a fictitious character; any resemblance to one such person is coincidental and unintentional.

GOALS:

Upon completion of this Workshop, the reader will:

➤ Expand on Workshop 2 by exploring the connection between cultural worldviews and mental models

➤ Explore how mental models drive behavior, and examine personal mental models that may pose challenges in intercultural situations

➤ Understand the rationale for and initiate the process of shifting mental models in order to achieve better individual and team results

➤ Understand how stereotypes drive behavior

➤ Explore the role and effects of self-fulfilling prophecy

WHAT IS A MENTAL MODEL?

> " Like a pane of glass framing and subtly distorting our vision, mental models determine what we see. "
>
> —Peter Senge

Mental models, a phrase first coined by Scottish psychologist Kenneth Craik in the 1940s, are psychological representations of reality, and as such, they constitute images, assumptions, and stories about people, cultures, objects, and events.[1] Established by a past event, experience, or teaching, they serve, going forward, as filters through which we see, interpret, and respond to the world—limiting us to familiar ways of thinking and behaving.[2] Fortunately, mental models have the *potential* to evolve through ongoing learning and interaction with new individuals and environments.

Individuals within a given culture *may* share similar models for common objects (e.g., associating food with chicken and beef) and events (e.g., associating white dresses and close family with weddings), while individuals from other cultures often have very different mental models for those same objects (e.g., associating food with monkeys and spiders) and events (e.g., associating weddings with red dresses and entire village attendance). Despite having a shared culture, it should be noted that it is still possible for individuals to see things differently and therefore, have different mental models; this is most visible on occasions when two people provide two completely different accounts after having witnessed the same event (e.g., "The new manager didn't know how to handle the conflict, and so she said nothing to the two employees" versus "The manager recognized the need

for these individuals to establish a positive working relationship, and so she gave them the opportunity to sort it out themselves").

Mental models play a powerful role in shaping:

➤ What we see and hear[3]

➤ What we feel

➤ What we do[4]

Mental models influence what we see and hear as they determine what information we pay attention to and what information we take in. Two types of perception error include **top-down bias**—the tendency to allow existing knowledge to bias thoughts and actions (e.g., Jane's preconceived notions about New Yorkers and cultural difference led her to avoid interactions with colleagues), and **confirmation bias**—the tendency to seek evidence that confirms, rather than negates, original beliefs and decisions (e.g., Jane most likely considered her encounters with "confrontational" big city or ethnically different individuals to be further evidence that one should avoid cultural difference).

Mental models also fuel our emotions and shape our attitudes. Jane Smith most likely associated negative feelings with life in New York City. Her friends and family warned that the move might not be a good decision, and as a result, her preestablished bias about New York City culture and its diverse people ultimately ensured that she realized and experienced those negative emotions. In the end, her attitude resulted in ineffectiveness in her role.

Jane's ineffectiveness in her role illustrates the third point, which is that mental models guide our behavior and determine the action we will take. A more generalized example of mental models influencing action follows: If we believe that people are basically good, we might be more inclined to be nice to strangers, trust our neighbors, leave our doors unlocked, and be more social. Yet, if we believe people are fundamentally evil, we may be more inclined to lock our doors tight, be wary of strangers, take a long time to trust others, and surround ourselves with a very small circle of friends. Jane Smith's preconceptions most likely did not associate very many positive attributes with New Yorkers, and therefore, her actions did not support the building of relationships with others.

Mental models do have the potential to be helpful as they can help us to:

➤ Organize our knowledge

➤ Quickly retrieve relevant information

➤ Make sense of and create order in a complex world

➤ Comprehend new situations easier and predict what we might expect about how things work

➤ Solve problems

The challenges that mental models present, however, are equally significant, especially in relation to intercultural effectiveness. Specifically:

➤ Mental models are self-perpetuating. For example, Jane Smith created a vicious cycle for herself. She did not believe that New York City was a good place to live because of the degree of cultural difference she would face. Her beliefs led her to take a particular course of action. This course of action resulted in her ineffectiveness and isolation. In her isolation and discomfort, she found confirmation of her initial belief that New York City was not a good place to live.

➤ Mental models, because they are often invisible to us, lead us to think our beliefs are based on truth and fact, and so we never question them.

➤ Mental models interfere with our ability to see the world in new and different ways and to identify and integrate new information—in other words, to learn.

➤ Mental models often lead to action that is based, in large part, on faulty thought processes.

➤ Mental models often take the form of deeply held, yet unfounded assumptions or beliefs about others.

➤ Mental models serve as a powerful vehicle for the perpetuation of stereotypes from one generation to the next.

Because mental models tend to exist outside of our awareness, they are seldom tested or challenged. In an intercultural context, actions resulting from outdated mental models are difficult to counter because the underlying thoughts defining the mental model are seldom verbally articulated. These thoughts are, nonetheless, *indirectly* communicated, as they tend to result in **microinequities**—subtle intercultural or interracial offenses. (Macroinequities, on the other hand, are reflected in broader institutional offenses, such as the Jim Crow laws that existed in the south.) Jane Touhey describes microinequities as small events that are covert, unintentional, hard to prove, and often unrecognized by the perpetrator, although she also points out that they "may be small in nature, but not trivial in the overall cumulative effect"[5].

Individuals perceive microinequities in "small," yet common offenses such as:

➤ Americans ignoring the foreigner on the team because he/she speaks little English.

➤ Male managers consistently interrupting female managers whenever they speak.

➤ A man proposing an idea already suggested by a woman and getting greater recognition for it.

➤ White Americans failing to make eye contact with people of color in the group, even when they initiate dialogue or pose a direct question.

As individuals belonging to groups lower on the **social hierarchy** (an informal construct representing the varying levels of power based on gender, ethnicity, racial group, and other classifications) are more likely to experience bias and discrimination, they often develop a keen ability to detect microinequities. When they do perceive one has occurred, they tend to speculate about the specific thought process or mental model that preceded the offending behavior, and end up struggling over whether or not to address what so far has mostly taken place in an unspoken arena.

We can only become aware of our mental models if we first have the desire, and then are encouraged, trained, and supported in doing so. Perhaps the motivation to develop such a desire can come from understanding that faulty mental models reflect most negatively on *us* when we speak and act from them. Faulty mental models communicate a lack of intelligence or social finesse, minimize credibility, and thwart the development of effective intercultural relationships. The implications for instructors, counselors, and other professionals whose effectiveness ultimately depends on the ability to establish positive working relationships with individuals from diverse backgrounds are significant.

Mental Models Illustrated

On the subject of marriage . . .

Men think: ball and chain; wedding; wife; friendship; commitment; family; children; partnership; shackles; forever; control; prison; love; togetherness; change; pain; fighting; problems; growing old; no more dating

Women think: security; wedding celebration; family; love; happiness; baby; companionship; children; commitment; hard work; financial support; personal growth; support; husband; tradition

On the subject of affirmative action . . .

Whites think: handouts; reverse discrimination; unfair advantage; Martin Luther King; Equal Opportunity Act; school busing; integration

Non-Whites think: equalizer; balancer; justice; right; good; help; not enough; better future; progress; stigma

Unfortunately, most of us underestimate just how much we rely on preexisting information and stereotypes to guide our interactions with others and just how emotionally tied to them we really are. Invested in our mental models, we resist acknowledging or modifying them even we encounter conflicting data or new information. **Perceptual defense** describes the process whereby a person's emotions screen out large blocks of information perceived to pose a threat to existing values and beliefs.[6] Making sense of conflicting information, it seems, can be emotionally challenging, especially if we first developed the mental models at a young age. Fortunately, training and support from experienced coaches, teachers, and counselors can help us to develop more constructive mental models.

As with so many other things, awareness is only the first step. Once we are aware of our mental models, we may still be unsure how to go about changing our behaviors and attitudes. Following are some tips to guide the use of mental models in a constructive way:

➢ Be aware that mental models are **tacit**.[7] They tend to exist outside your awareness until you look for them, and yet they play a powerful role in guiding your actions and emotions.

➢ Make a concerted effort to examine your specific mental models closely.

➢ Identify areas where your mental models are likely to negatively impact others at work or in your community.

➢ Slow down your thinking long enough to question the rationality and basis of your thoughts, and you will discover the underlying assumptions influencing your thoughts and actions.

➢ Reflect on conflicts or other situations that failed to go as well as you wanted and examine them by examining the mental models that may have been operating at the time.

- Replace faulty mental models with more constructive ones—those based on more accurate or specific information.

- Continually seek "fresh material" with which to evolve your mental models.

- Inquire about the perspectives of others in a nonjudgmental way.

Since mental models drive our feelings and behaviors, we cannot change our actions or attitudes without first revisiting and modifying those that do not serve us or others well. Fortunately, researchers have found that we can change even long-held, deep-seated beliefs if, over time, we work to modify short-term everyday models as the opportunities arise.

Should you encounter individuals who seem to be operating from different mental models, here are some steps you can take to promote mutual understanding:

- Recognize that others may not be aware of mental models.

- Inquire about their views, as a means of understanding their frame of reference.

- Share the assumptions and information underlying your own mental models.

- Be willing to have your assumptions and mental models questioned and perhaps even challenged.

- Guide others through the process of examining their own mental models more closely so that you might collaborate in identifying any information gaps or potentially faulty reasoning.

> " The core task of this discipline is bringing mental models to the surface, to explore and talk about them with minimal defensiveness—to help us see the pane of glass, see its impact on our lives, and find ways to re-form the glass by creating new mental models that serve us better in the world. "
>
> —Peter Senge

Exploring a Mental Model

Have you ever explored a mental model? As you read the following labels, make your mental models visible by free-associating whatever comes to mind (as demonstrated in the sidebar illustrating mental models for marriage and affirmative action). Try not to censor your thoughts. Write down whatever comes to mind. This list is for your eyes only.

Executives

Single, working mothers

Homeless people

Salespeople

Immigrants

Prisoners

Americans

Review your associations for each of the labels. Reflect on the following:

- Do your mental models positively or negatively influence your perspectives on each group?

_____

_____

_____

Activity 3.1

> How might these associations shape your attitudes and guide your behavior if you were to interact with each of these people?

_____

_____

_____

> How have you responded in the past to new information that does not fit with your existing mental models? How would you like to respond going forward?

_____

_____

LADDERS OF INFERENCE

Mental models often lead to what Chris Argyris identified as "ladders of inference," mental pathways of ever-increasing abstraction, resulting in misguided beliefs, conclusions, and actions.[8] The climb happens quickly and most of us are not even aware that we made such leaps. The only external evidence to indicate that the process has taken place is the conclusion, statement, or action taken as a result of the preexisting mental model.

Ladders of Inference Illustrated

On vacation in Miami, Florida, I met a Caucasian couple from Brooklyn, New York. They were about 15 years older than my husband (Caucasian) and I (Latina, person of color). They, unlike us, had been to Miami several times over the years and so they began to express their amazement about the extent to which, in their opinion, Miami blossomed. "You should have seen this place a few years ago," the woman said. "It looked like Harlem!" No sooner did these words come out of her mouth than the woman gasped, covered her mouth with one hand, and in an apologetic tone directed at me, said "No offense!" Clearly, her mental model for "Harlem" was a negative one.

Confused, I stood silent for a moment, reviewing our conversation up to that point and trying to pinpoint exactly what I might have said to indicate that I was from Harlem, which I was not. It was then that it dawned on me that this woman, unaware

©GETTY IMAGES

Where you go with your information depends on your use of ladders.

she did so, climbed the ladder of inference. In doing so, she made a series of incorrect assumptions, each leading her further up the ladder and toward the final conclusion that I was from Harlem or somehow had ties, emotional or other, to Harlem.

Deconstructing the Ladder of Inference

Although the ladder does begin with directly observable data (e.g., skin color), mental models quickly spring into action, filtering and interpreting this data. We begin making connections that increasingly build from our own preexisting ideas, rather than the original hard data. Healthy mental models help us to quickly make sense of new information, relate to others, and draw appropriate conclusions. It is important to understand that faulty mental models, on the other hand, result in inappropriate conclusions and actions based on inaccurate information that *we ourselves have created*.

What might the woman's ladder of inference have looked like in the above example?

Others suspect we have faulty mental models when our conclusions or actions do not make sense given all available or observable data. It seems we are more likely to apply faulty mental models when interacting with other social and cultural groups. Cognitive psychologists have identified varying patterns in perception, resulting in in-group versus out-group mental models, which fuel the all too common "us versus them" mentality. When interacting with members of different social or cultural groups, we assign less favorable characteristics to them and attribute poor performance to internal factors, such as innate ability or character. We attribute their positive performance, however, to external factors, such as luck, the environment, or people around them. When it comes to assessment of others more similar to us, the opposite occurs; we have a tendency to assign generally positive characteristics to others sharing our social or cultural backgrounds and attribute poor performance to external factors and positive performance to internal factors.

LINKING MENTAL MODELS AND STEREOTYPES

The meanings and interpretations we contribute as we climb up our ladders of inference are often the result of stereotypes we knowingly, or unknowingly, engage.

Stereotypes are the result of fixed impressions, exaggerated or preconceived ideas about particular social groups, usually based solely on physical appearance. They are:

➤ Simplified ideas, whether perceived as positive or negative, about people of another group

➤ Culturally learned

➤ Overgeneralizations that are not accurate for every individual, and often most individuals, in a group

➤ Designed to enhance our own self-identity[9]

➤ The foundation for prejudice and discrimination[10]

➤ Obstacles in getting to know others for whom they are versus whom we think they might be

Firmly established at a young age, these ideas remain as most mental models—untested and unchallenged. For example, by three years of age, children begin labeling by race (as they are taught to define it). By seven years of age, they begin to draw information from stereotypes in their application of racial labels. Common sources for these early mental models include parents, other family members, educators, peers, and the media. Unfortunately, those who have deeply held stereotypes tend to seek information to support them, rather than test new information. As we tend to resist information that does not fit with our existing mental models, we look outside

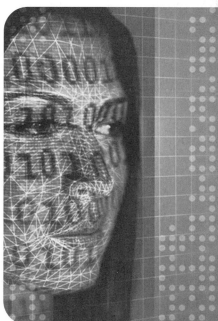

©CHAD BAKER/PHOTODISC/GETTY IMAGES

Stereotypes distort your view of others.

ourselves, rather than within, to find reasons for any discrepancies we encounter. It is easier to blame the individual who does not support our preexisting mental models and therefore meet our expectation for consistency, than it is to look within, revisit our mental model, and test its validity.

"Positive" stereotypes merit special attention, as many individuals will argue that this particular brand of stereotype is not harmful. I once worked with an Asian male who passionately resented the "positive" stereotype "Asians are smart." "What if you're not?" he would ask. "What kind of pressure is that for a kid growing up, expected to be something he just is not." "Positive" stereotypes, like negative stereotypes, have the potential to result in negative self-image, stress, mental illness, pressure to conform, and ineffective intercultural interactions.

Exploring Use of Stereotypes in Classic Films

Many movies, particularly classic movies, employed the use of stereotypes to portray men, women, immigrants, and a variety of cultural and racial groups. Select a popular classic movie of your choice, preferably one you have already watched or want to watch. Conduct an online search for reviews or essays that address the movie's portrayal of its characters (try entering: "movie name" + stereotypes). Reflect on the questions below.

➤ How does the movie make use of stereotypes?

_____

_____

_____

_____

➤ Which social or cultural groups are stereotyped?

_____

_____

_____

_____

➤ What are the stereotypes?

_____

_____

_____

_____

➤ What might portrayal of these characters indicate about the time period in which the movie was made?

_____

_____

_____

_____

➤ Do these stereotypes exist today? If so, how have they changed if at all?

_____

_____

_____

_____

Media wields great power in its ability to perpetuate stereotypes. As you read books, newspapers, and magazines and watch television, movies, and commercials, adopt a new pair of lens. Consider how the media continues, even today, to utilize, perpetuate, and teach stereotypes through the many written and visual vehicles we access on a daily basis.

Stereotypes are pervasive and powerful examples of mental models in our society. As such, they provide a constant backdrop for our thoughts and actions. Many workshop attendees proudly proclaim, at first, that they themselves do not personally hold stereotypes of others. Witnessing the ease with which a group can generate and collectively agree on the commonality of many specific stereotypes associated with a wide range of social/cultural groups quickly demonstrates, however, just how pervasive these mental models really are. Effectively communicating across cultures requires a commitment to being more purposeful in soliciting information from others as well as a concerted effort to appreciate others as individuals—each with his/her own unique ways of viewing and interacting with the world. If we can manage this, only then might we be more successful in mitigating the effects of stereotypes that we, like all Americans, have inherited.

©ANGUS PLUMMER/ISTOCKPHOTO

Our ideas about others help to shape their outcomes.

SELF-FULFILLING PROPHECY: THE POWER OF EXPECTATION

Stereotypes are not only harmful to the individuals they target. Societies, organizations, teams, and other individuals not in the target group also collectively experience the negative effects of stereotypes. This stems in large part from another psychological phenomenon first identified and coined as the **Pygmalion Effect**, or self-fulfilling prophecy. Over the past five

decades, professor and researcher Dr. Robert Rosenthal has performed experiments and studies in various settings, validating and documenting evidence of the powerful effects of expectations on performance. His research provides the scientific evidence behind the cliché "what we think becomes so."

Beliefs establish and communicate either positive or negative expectations (e.g., girls do not do well in math, artistic people are quirky). Although these beliefs may not be true for a particular individual at the beginning of the relationship with his manager, he/she is likely to ultimately behave as if it were. Implications for managers include:

➤ Establish a climate of support—Verbally and nonverbally communicate the expectation that all employees will do well; nonverbals such as tone of voice, eye contact, facial expression, and body posture will communicate either negative or positive expectations.

➤ Let your actions speak louder than words—Managers who hold positive expectations of their employees are more friendly, supportive, and accepting, and give more attention, assistance, and encouragement.

➢ Reward results and support development—Managers who hold positive expectations provide more feedback, helpful guidance, and encourage and communicate higher performance expectations.

We are seldom aware that we reinforce behavior that complies with our initial expectation, shun behavior that contradicts the expectation, and attribute

CASE STUDIES[11]

In 1969, a classroom experiment tested instructor expectations on student performance. Researchers arbitrarily designated 20 percent of the class as "bloomers," students showing promise and heightened capability. Random selection of "bloomers" ensured the outcome would be a true assessment of instructor expectation. **Result:** "Bloomers" scored a total of four points more in total IQ than the rest of their classmates, demonstrating that an instructor's expectation is sufficient enough to affect student performance, that those who are expected to do well are more likely to do well, and that expectations alone exert a strong influence on the manner in which we interact with others. There was, however, another surprising finding: Those expected to do well overall—all fast track students—were *favorably* viewed when their scores increased; on the other hand, those who were not expected to do well—those on the slow track—were *unfavorably* viewed when their scores increased. This powerful finding reinforced the idea that because of our fixed mental models and stereotypes, we prefer that others behave as we expect them to.

In 1975, a similar study conducted in the work environment found similar results and provided implications for managers, who were shocked to learn that expectation alone had influenced their interactions when they sincerely believed they had treated all employees the same.

unexpected positive results to external factors such as luck, mentors, or token status. Nonetheless, these tendencies have a particularly powerful effect on another phenomenon, called the **Galatea Effect**. Whereas the Pygmalion Effect links *external* expectations with individual performance outcomes, the Galatea Effect links *internal* expectations with performance outcomes.[12] When expectations are **internalized**—adopted and personally held by the target group or individual—teams, organizations, and society as a whole fail to reap the benefits of fully empowered, fully engaged members who are able to realize their potential.

> " 'We're running as an economy at 30 percent efficiency' because so many workers are not contributing as much as they could.
>
> —Steve Bates "

Healthy self-image is critical to productive membership in groups; therefore, stereotypes present a very real threat to organizational and societal performance. It is important to remember that the cues we provide regarding our expectations and stereotypes can be subtle. Challenging the negative stereotypes we have learned, as well as those we encounter in our work environment, can ensure that higher expectations of all individuals result in greater engagement and higher performance.

> " The difference between a lady and flower girl isn't how she behaves, it's how she's treated.
>
> —Eliza Dolittle from the movie *Pygmalion* "

Interactive Group Activity: Exploring Personal Experiences with Stereotypes and Self-Fulfilling Prophecy

Part A

Take a few minutes to consider your thoughts in response to the following questions:

➤ How have you personally experienced stereotypes? Describe the situation and context.

_____
_____
_____

➤ What was your response to being stereotyped? What challenges did these stereotypes present?

_____
_____
_____

➤ Can you identify any examples of self-fulfilling prophecy from your experience? If so, describe the situation and context. What were the associated costs or benefits?

_____
_____
_____

➤ How might you begin to examine the mental models guiding your interactions with others?

_____
_____
_____

➤ What is one mental model you currently are aware you hold, which you would like to shift?

_____
_____
_____

Part B

➤ Working in small groups, reflect on and discuss your responses to the questions in Part A.

➤ As you share your responses, be sure to actively listen to other group members and ask open-ended questions that will solicit helpful information. Remember that the cues to our own mental models and expectations are often subtle; accordingly, make a conscious effort to remain aware of your nonverbals such as tone of voice, eye contact, and body posture.

Part C

Review the activity by responding to the following questions:

➤ What did you learn?

_____
_____
_____

➤ As the group shared different experiences, what did you find most challenging?

_____
_____
_____

➤ What were the commonalities?

_____
_____
_____

➤ How did the group respond to differences?

_____
_____
_____

SHIFTING MENTAL MODELS FOR BETTER RESULTS

> ❝ We will never be able to walk the same path that another person walks, but maybe we can think more carefully about where we are stepping. ❞
>
> —Anonymous

The key to shifting faulty mental models is to slow down our thought process. Conflicts and encounters with different perspectives provide perfect opportunities to revisit our mental models and confirm that we are not operating from those that may be faulty or outdated.

➤ Actively investigate your mental models because they constantly guide your actions and emotions.

➤ Avoid making erroneous assumptions or drawing inaccurate conclusions by remaining aware of ladders of inference, asking more questions, and checking your facts.

➤ Slow down your thinking long enough to question the rationality and basis of your thoughts so you can discover the underlying assumptions.

➤ Reflect on previous conflicts or other situations that failed to go as well as you wanted and examine the mental models that may have been operating at the time.

➤ Replace faulty models with more constructive ones.

➤ Continually seek "fresh material."

Becoming more in tune with our mental models requires enhancement of particular skills such as inquiry, empathy, and self-monitoring. It also requires greater reflection so that we might identify the theories we think we ascribe to (all men are created equal) versus those on which we tend to act (women do not belong in the workplace). No amount of learning can take place until those gaps have been identified and resolved.[13] Awareness of such gaps greatly enhances learning and should therefore not be met with negative self-judgment or discouragement.

Remember also that others can be of great help in reflecting. Inviting others to share their perceptions with you and opening yourself up to feedback and challenge will ensure that your mental models are refreshed and renewed—incorporating new, accurate information on a regular basis.

 ## Online Research—Using Keywords

Access additional resources and information with the following online search terms: cognitive psychology, Galatea Effect, in-group versus out-group bias, ladders of inference, mental models, Pygmalion Effect, self-fulfilling prophecy, and stereotypes.

Some specific resources for cognition and perception studies include the *Behavioral and Brain Sciences Journal, Canadian Journal of Psychology, Cognition, Cognitive Psychology, Developmental Psychology, Psychological Science,* and *Trends in Cognitive Sciences.*

Activity 3.4

Points to Remember

➤ Mental models are psychological representations of reality, and as such, they constitute images, assumptions, and stories about people, cultures, objects, and events; cultures often hold very different mental models.

➤ Mental models shape what we see, hear, feel, and do.

➤ Ladders of inference, although based on observable data, result in assumptions and logical leaps that increasingly represent our mental models, rather than reality.

➤ Stereotypes, whether perceived to be positive or negative, are oversimplified generalizations and seldom capture all, or even most, individuals within the target group.

➤ The Pygmalion Effect represents a very real link between external expectations and individual/group performance; a related phenomenon, the Galatea Effect, represents the link between internal expectations and performance.

Endnotes

1. P.M. Senge, A. Kleiner, C. Roberts, R.B. Ross, & B.J. Smith, *The Fifth Discipline Fieldbook: Strategies and Tools for Building a Learning Organization*, Doubleday, 1994

2. P.M. Senge, Mental Models: Putting strategic ideas into practice, *Planning Review*, March–April, 1992, Vol. 20 No. 2

3. J. Cromley, Learning to Think, Learning to Learn: What the science of thinking and learning has to offer adult education, National Institute for Literacy, 2000

4. T. Liebig, Mental Models, SGZZ Systems Thinking, Published online

5. D. Lang, *3 Ways Corporations Can Combat Cluelessness*, DiversityInc Media, January, 2004

6. S. McShane & M.A. Van Glinow, Organization Behavior: Emerging realities for the workplace revolution, Chapters 3, 4, The McGraw-Hill Companies, Inc., 2003

7. P.M. Senge, A. Kleiner, C. Roberts, R.B. Ross, & B.J. Smith, op. cit.

8. P.M. Senge, A. Kleiner, C. Roberts, R.B. Ross, & B.J. Smith, op. cit.

9. S. McShane & M.A. Van Glinow, op. cit.

10. S. McShane & M.A. Van Glinow, op. cit.

11. CRM Films, *Productivity and the Self-Fulfilling Prophecy: The Pygmalion Effect*, Second Edition

12. Ibid.

13. P.M. Senge, op.cit.

ESTABLISHING KEY COMMUNICATION SKILLS

©SUSAN LEVAN/PHOTODISC/
GETTY IMAGES

Do you mean what I mean when I say . . .?

Misfit or Miscommunication: An Intercultural Interview

Workshop 4 marks a transition from the awareness-building segments to the skills-building part of this workbook with a review of effective communication skills.

Meredith Chesterfield was transferred from one of the company's European offices and asked to head the blossoming U.S. office based in New York. If they were going to meet their aggressive goals, she thought, they were going to need talented staff that could quickly get up to speed and deliver. As head of the New York division, her job was to make sure she successfully attracted and retained that talent. A well-respected colleague submitted the résumé of someone he promised would be an immediate asset to her team, so Meredith quickly scheduled the interview.

Jan Chen, an Asian candidate, was clearly intelligent, but she was very soft spoken. In response to Meredith's direct and challenging interview style, Jan provided indirect, vague responses, which Meredith had difficulty making heads or tails of. She seemed to have difficulty answering specific questions such as "What are your greatest strengths and accomplishments?" and "How do you like to be managed?"

Meredith found Jan's unwillingness to maintain direct eye contact or smile somewhat disconcerting. Before the interview was even over, Meredith found herself struggling over what she was going to tell her colleague. She was disappointed; Jan had not demonstrated the leadership qualities her colleague had been so enthusiastic about. After putting more thought into it, however, Meredith decided that she understood the real problem: Jan had not been interested in joining the company from the start! Perhaps Jan had simply been polite in honoring the interview, which came at the suggestion of Meredith's colleague, who was also Jan's ex-boss. Suddenly, all the other nonverbal cues made sense. Meredith settled on this conclusion and decided that the solution was simple; she would send Jan Chen a letter thanking her for her time and wishing her well. Meredith was also sure to follow up with her colleague and let him know that Jan Chen was not interested.

When Jan first received the letter, she was excited. As she began to read the letter, however, she soon realized that they were not extending an offer, and she was shocked. The interview had gone so well, she thought. She contacted her ex-boss for some insight, but he only informed her that the company said she was not interested. She felt even more confused and again reflected on the interview, how she had been polite, professional, and not overly aggressive. Had she not demonstrated the appropriate level of respect for someone in a position of authority? Did her résumé not clearly show the results of her work? Confident that the rejection was not due to anything she herself had done, Jan ultimately decided that the company was probably just not ready for diversity.

Upon completion of this Workshop, the reader will:

➤ Define *effective communication*

➤ Identify the four parts to effective communication

➤ Understand the significance of culture in verbal and nonverbal communication

➤ Recognize empathy and validation as critical intercultural communication tools

COMMUNICATING WITH CLARITY

Effective communication—the art and technique of using words and nonverbals effectively to impart and/or exchange information or ideas—generally requires incorporation of the following four elements: active listening, inquiry, advocacy, and reflection. A brief discussion of each is provided in the following sections.

Effective Communication Requirement 1: Active Listening

> "
> God gave us two ears but only one mouth, a divine indication that we should listen twice as much as we talk.
> "
> –Anonymous

There is often confusion between the terms *hearing* and *listening*; generally the former is mistaken for the latter. An old friend used to joke about a test she would consistently give to people who did not listen. She would identify a dazed look in their eyes and then ask, "Did you hear what I just said?" She was always amazed to discover, that like robots, these individuals would unfailingly repeat in a monotonous tone, almost verbatim what

she had said only a few minutes ago. "I've come to the conclusion that we're born with tape recorders in our heads," she would say, "but it doesn't mean we ever really listen to one another."

Hearing is defined as follows: to perceive (sound) by the ear[1]. Given this simple definition, we can conclude that processing, reflection, and response do not necessarily accompany hearing. **Listening**, on the other hand, is defined as follows: to pay attention[2]. **Active listening** goes one step further by prescribing a specific approach to paying attention and outlines three steps to effective listening:

1. Providing appropriate verbal and nonverbal cues communicates that the message has been received, and may prompt the speaker to continue (e.g., "hmm," "yes," "uh-huh," nodding, eye contact).

2. **Paraphrasing**—restating what we have heard in our own words as a means of clarifying a particular message—ensures that we have received and interpreted the intended message clearly. To maximize effectiveness, paraphrasing should address not only content but the associated context and emotions as well. In addition, it allows the speaker of the original message an opportunity to respond (e.g., "I think I hear you saying that you don't enjoy presenting in front of your peers because you fear you are being evaluated. Is that correct?").

3. Broader in scope, summarizing what has been said provides an additional check for understanding and serves as a periodic recap. Conversations often take many twists and turns, with one or both individuals going off on tangents and risking the possibility of losing the initial thread of thought. Periodically summarizing what has been said enables both individuals to review what has been shared up to

that point, and makes sure that they remain on the same page.

Challenges to active listening include the following:

1. External "noise," such as accents or improper use of vocabulary or grammar by others, may thwart our ability to comprehend the message.

2. Internal "noise" presented by our own filters (e.g., mental models, worldviews, values, expectations) often distort the message we receive.

3. Personal challenges may prohibit us from actively listening (e.g., feeling rushed, relying on negative stereotypes, having a lack of interest).

4. How we listen is culturally influenced. For example, in some cultures, eye contact is not always a requirement. In fact, it may even be considered unacceptable behavior (e.g., in conversations where there is a clear difference in power such as that between a boss and an employee). Failing to understand that others may demonstrate active listening in different ways creates additional communication challenges.

Although many internal and external challenges may exist, we can create opportunities to promote shared understanding by incorporating the three parts to effective listening: giving cues, paraphrasing, and summarizing. In this way, we collaborate in the discussion process rather than remain a passive participant. Exploring varying cultural norms, specifically pertaining to listening, can heighten our awareness of American norms as well as the many cultural variations that exist.

Effective Communication Requirement 2: Inquiry

Inquiry—the process of soliciting relevant information that will promote clarity and understanding—serves as an especially

Do you see yourself reflected in any of these listening personalities?

➤ **"The Interrupter"** seldom lets other individuals finish their thoughts, often erroneously completing the speaker's sentences based on his/her assumptions.

➤ **"The Fidgeter"** may hear, but body language indicates that he/she is not fully interested or listening (e.g., the individual who keeps looking at his/her watch as you speak).

➤ **"The One-Upper"** views conversation as a competition and provides one of his/her own stories or perspectives in response to each one provided by the other speaker; the result is two separate lines of conversation.

➤ **"The Chess Player,"** rather than listen, stays busy thinking about what he/she is going to say in response; this individual tends to skip the paraphrasing and summarizing steps of active listening, and may overuse cues as a means of rushing others along.

➤ **"The Floater"** repeatedly floats off during conversation, visibly daydreaming, turning his/her attention to other things or even walking away mid-sentence.

➤ **"The Ethnocentric"** believes everyone feels and sees things in the same way, and therefore, fails to identify cultural difference; this individual, as a result, has a tendency to offend or arouse sensitivities when speaking, asking questions or interpreting messages from others who may differ along one or more cultural dimensions.

useful tool in intercultural communication because it provides direct access to the speaker's particular thought process, context, and/or mental models.

Most likely, many of us have encountered individuals who make improper use of inquiry. I refer to these individuals as "The Interrogators." Misunderstanding the purpose and role of inquiry, these individuals pose question after question in an attempt to convey curiosity and interest. The result is usually an exhausted individual on the receiving end of the interrogator's many questions.

Effective use of inquiry incorporates a selective and balanced use of both open-ended and closed questions. **Open-ended questions** require more than a yes/no response and encourage the speaker to elaborate on a given point (e.g., What can you tell me about your experience in Cambodia?). **Closed questions** can be answered with a simple yes/no response (e.g., Do you come from Laos?). The inquirer must carefully choose the questions that he will ask in order to reflect the true nature of his/her interest and accurately probe key areas that will be sure to provide additional insight.

Challenges to effective inquiry include the following:

1. Inquiry requires practice. As we have discussed, ineffective inquiry may resemble interrogation. It may also appear to others to be insincere or communicate a lack of judgment.

2. The questions an individual chooses to ask or deems appropriate to answer is again culturally determined. Understanding cultural norms and noting the topics that are considered safe for discussion can help us to steer clear of unintentional offenses.

3. Internal biases and faulty mental models may rear their ugly heads in the form of questions that are built upon incorrect or stereotypical assumptions (e.g., Upon seeing his Latina host's beautiful home, an Asian guest asks how she managed to do so well financially, relying on stereotypes and never considering that she may have been born into a family of wealth). Pausing to reflect and asking ourselves whether our questions are based on assumption or fact can prevent us from making this kind of error.

4. Recognizing that cultural norms often prescribe fixed responses to common

questions can prepare us to meet the needs of both our cultural guests and our own needs. For example, Americans respond to the question "How are you?" with a simple, even if dishonest response, while individuals from other cultures often take a literal approach and surprise us by providing elaborate responses, detailing any number of ailments when we were only expecting them to say "Fine." "Can I offer you something to eat?" may in some cultures be met with a polite "No, thank you" at least three times before etiquette dictates that they can finally accept.

Used effectively, inquiry enables us to explore the other individual's worldviews, mental models, and perspectives and results in greater collaboration and appreciation for the intercultural communication process.

Effective Communication Requirement 3: Advocacy

Advocacy describes the act of articulating our position, perspective, or opinion. Effectively advocating requires that in addition to stating our position or perspective, we make visible to ourselves and to others the mental models that guide our reasoning and assumptions (e.g., That's an interesting thought. As a woman, I have always considered traveling alone to be a risky endeavor.). It also requires that we enable or invite others to respond to our views and assumptions, that we actively listen to and inquire about their perspectives, and that we remain open-minded to the possibility of learning and shifting our points of view based on this new information (e.g., Have your experiences led you to a different conclusion?). Anything less is a mere attempt by one or both parties to simply muscle the other individual into "seeing things his or her own way," clearly, a very ethnocentric approach to dialogue.

Challenges to effective advocacy include the following:

1. Effectively advocating in an intercultural context requires acknowledgment of varying cultural worldviews. In other words, it is helpful to always recognize that what you believe to be right, true, or good is driven by your own experience within your particular cultural environment and that it is seldom synonymous with universal truths that apply equally in cross-cultural contexts.

2. Unless we demonstrate a willingness to hear, listen to, and investigate other perspectives (what others are advocating), we undermine the credibility of our own perspectives.

3. Ineffectively advocating one's position may lead others to interpret or view our actions as challenging, provoking of conflict, or at the very least, judgmental.

Effective advocacy enables us to present our thinking to others—what we feel and believe and why. As such, it provides an opportunity for both parties to thoroughly explore and understand commonalities as well as the very real and specific ways in which the parties may differ.

Effective Communication Requirement 4: Reflection

Peter Senge describes **reflection** as slowing down our thinking processes in order to become more aware of our mental models[3]. Reflection plays an important role in our ability to establish and utilize effective communication practices, particularly in an intercultural context. Effectively engaging in dialogue with others requires that we first reflect on *ourselves*—noting the reactions, emotions, and assumptions we experience as we communicate with and listen to others. Second, it requires that we reflect on and remain aware of *others*—the reactions,

emotions, and assumptions they may be experiencing in response to our words and actions. Third, it requires that we reflect on the communication *process* itself, that we ask important questions such as the following:

➤ "Are emotions an invisible but nonetheless influential part of the process here?"

➤ "Are assumptions on either party's side serving as obstacles to understanding?"

➤ "Am I being understood? If not, is there another way I might deliver my message more effectively?"

Challenges to effective reflection include the following:

1. Our willingness or tendency to reflect may be precluded by an ethnocentric ideology, which presumes that others think, feel, or believe as we do. Unfortunately, as we discussed in Workshop 2, in the attempts to address social equality, American ideologies have for some time reflected the expectation of a melting pot—minimizing the importance of cultural difference and erroneously creating the illusion of sameness.

2. Culturally, Americans tend to value **extraversion**—turning our attention and energy to the outer world—over **introversion**—turning our attention and energy inward toward the thoughts, concepts, and ideas that help us to make sense of the world around us. This often translates into a direct challenge to our willingness and ability to develop the core skill that is reflection.

3. In the absence of reflection, we react rather than respond. Reactions are fertile ground for ethnocentric behaviors, thoughts, and words, further complicating and potentially impeding the intercultural communication process.

4. We forget that our worldviews are limited, acknowledging only the things that reflect our own background, knowledge, experience, and education.

5. We pass judgment on others, which only reflects our own limited worldviews rather than any truths about the other individual.

6. We miss the opportunity to establish greater self-understanding and/or mutual understanding.

By incorporating reflection both during and after exchanges, we can eventually learn to communicate more authentically, conveying only those messages and thoughts we truly want to share, and doing so more clearly. Authentic communication promotes honest dialogue and collaborative discussion.

Together the four parts of effective communication—active listening, inquiry, advocacy, and reflection—create numerous possibilities for collaboration in dialogue.

Active listening, inquiry, and reflection play particularly critical roles in intercultural communication. Our ability to effectively hear, interpret, and respond to others who may hold different frameworks for understanding relies on our ability to first understand that we ourselves have a

Meanings assigned to nonverbal gestures may vary widely across cultures.

particular set of expectations and ways of interpreting the world, and that the expectations and interpretations of others may, and often do, significantly differ. With this awareness as a foundation, we can then utilize our active listening and inquiry skills to respond appropriately and to explore and understand other worldviews, mental models, and frameworks. Finally, developing an ability to effectively and appropriately advocate our perspectives can enable us to communicate our unique worldviews to others from a place of mutual inquiry and sharing, rather than from judgment and imposition.

Personal Communication SWOT Analysis

Part A
Review the four components of communication. Identify a recent conversation you may have had, particularly one that failed to go as you had planned. Reflect on that specific conversation and indicate how much time you spent on each of the four components by allocating percentages that total 100 percent.

Time spent actively listening as an Interrupter, Fidgeter, One-Upper, Chess Player, Floater, or Ethnocentric   _____

Time spent effectively inquiring   _____

Time spent interrogating   _____

Activity 4.1

Time spent effectively advocating   _____

Time spent pushing your viewpoint   _____

Time spent reflecting   _____

Total: _____ + _____ = 100%

How might a shift in allocation have created a different result?

_____
_____
_____
_____

Part B

SWOT Analysis is an assessment of Strengths, Weaknesses, Opportunities, and Threats. In this exercise, you will reflect on your general communication style and conduct your own SWOT analysis. Consider your percentage allocations in Part A and think about the following SWOT categories. Be sure to solicit input and/or feedback from others and compare them with your own comments.

Your communication **weaknesses**

_____
_____
_____

Where are there **opportunities** to improve your communication skills?

_____
_____
_____

What **threats** to your ability to improve your overall communication skills can you identify? To improve your intercultural communication skills?

_____
_____
_____
_____

Your communication **strengths**

_____
_____
_____
_____

©ANTONIO MO/PHOTODISC/GETTY IMAGES

Effective communication requires collaboration.

NONVERBAL COMMUNICATION AND CULTURE

> " There is an entire universe of behavior that is unexplored, unexamined, and very much taken for granted. It functions outside conscious awareness and in juxtaposition to words. "
>
> —Milton J. Bennett

Nonverbals—responses that convey meaning without the use of words—cannot be underestimated in their ability to influence communication and understanding, particularly when we consider that researchers estimate that nonverbals comprise between 80 and 90 percent of what gets communicated. Cultures vary widely in their use of nonverbals, as well as in the meanings they attribute to common gestures, facial expressions, or body language. One very important cultural difference is captured by the terms *low context* and *high context*.[4]

Low context cultures are reflected in the cliché "It's not what you say, but *how* you say it." These cultures communicate primarily via explicit code (i.e., reliance on words), which is further modified (often unconsciously) by indirect methods of communication such as nonverbals—gestures, eye contact, or physical space. Researchers categorize American culture as low context. An example of this preference can be found in the relatively high importance that American women and men tend to place on the words "I love you." In the workplace, low context cultures encourage and expect direct conversation between employees, even across organizational levels. An example here might be a subordinate saying "I don't think I can get that file to you by Friday" to a supervisor. Other low context cultures include Germanic and Scandinavian countries.

High context cultures, on the other hand, might be reflected in a modified version of the cliché "It's not what you say, but how you *show* it." These cultures stress indirect communication methods where most of the message is not found in the explicit code. They demand that individuals rely on inference and context to draw meaning from nonverbals, believing this to be a more credible method of conveying meaning. How something is said, by whom, to whom, when, where, and in what context become more important than what is said. Expanding on the previous example used to illustrate low context cultural preference, couples from high context cultures may place a greater emphasis on "showing" rather than speaking of their love. In the workplace, high context cultures understand that a subordinate will not verbally contradict or oppose a superior. An example here might contrast with the low context situation where an employee does not feel at liberty to say no to his boss and may, despite his/her concern over being able to deliver by Friday, say something such as "I will make every effort to have that in your hands by Friday" whether or not he/she actually can. High context cultures include African, East Asian, Mediterranean, Middle Eastern, and some Latin American countries.

Researchers have identified several categories of nonverbals along which cultures tend to differ:

➤ **Paralanguage** refers to the pitch, stress, volume, and speed used to convey messages. (For example, Northern Americans tend to associate various attributes to southerners because of their slower speech and vice versa.)

➤ **Kinesics** refers to use of body language. (For example, the use of sweeping hand gestures by many Greeks and Italians is considered overwhelming to those from East Asian cultures, where body movement is minimized.)

➤ **Haptics** refers to the use of touching. (For example, in many Latin cultures, touching expresses warmth and openness; in other European cultures, touching between strangers or acquaintances is frowned upon.)

➤ **Chronemics** refers to the use and meaning of time. (For example, in some cultures, lateness is a cause for insult; in others, it is accepted.)

➤ **Proxemics** refers to the perception and use of space. (For example, different cultures have different norms and protocols for seating arrangements, conversational distance, and personal space.)

These categories, like the broad areas of cultural difference reviewed in Workshop 2, often serve as pitfalls to understanding in the intercultural communication process.

Intercultural communication challenges include: missing nonverbal cues because they do not align with the norms and practices of our own culture; perceiving a cue where none was intended; and **ethnocentric interpretation**, which refers to the tendency to erroneously interpret the nonverbal cues provided by individuals of other cultures, within the context of our own culture.[5] While we need not necessarily "do as the Romans do" in an intercultural context, we are best served by understanding that communication norms and practices of other cultures often differ and then making sure that we effectively employ inquiry as a means of attaining access to the potentially different thought processes, mental models, and worldviews. In short, we must recognize (as demonstrated in Figure 4.1) that our particular cultural lens serves as a filter through which we create meaning and through which we interpret not only the words, but the nonverbal cues that others provide.

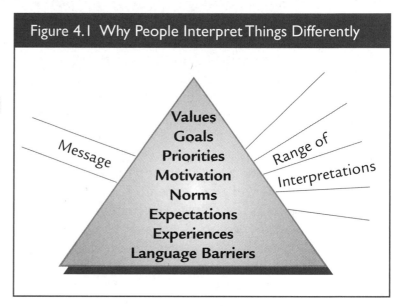

Figure 4.1 Why People Interpret Things Differently

Message

Values
Goals
Priorities
Motivation
Norms
Expectations
Experiences
Language Barriers

Range of Interpretations

Online Research— Meanings and Nonverbal Gestures

Did you know that

➤ Handing something to or touching others with your left may offend individuals from some middle eastern and Asian cultures.

➤ Showing the soles of shoes or feet is considered rude in India and Southeast Asia.

➤ Smiling can be a sign of embarrassment or confusion in some Asian cultures.

➤ Giving the American OK sign is equivalent to giving the middle finger in some Latin American countries.

➤ Crossing one's arms is a sign of arrogance in some Scandinavian countries.

Run a quick online search to identify other cultural differences in meanings attributed to nonverbal gestures.

TIP:

Entering "culture" + the specific gesture, expression, or body part you wish to research may yield more results that are directly relevant.

CRITICAL INTERCULTURAL COMMUNICATION TOOLS: EMPATHY AND VALIDATION

To best understand others, try walking a mile in their shoes.

Many of us upon encountering difference, find ourselves **sympathizing** (imagining and interpreting the thoughts, experiences, and perspectives of others from *our own* lens) rather than **empathizing** (attempting to understand the thoughts, experiences, and perspectives of others from *their own* perspectives).

For example, Americans may look at polygamy and think "How primitive, unfair, and immoral." We may sympathize with the women in these polygamous cultures and experience frustration, anger, and sadness, believing that we understand their situation. And yet, we have only succeeded in viewing their experience through the lens of our own culture, projecting our own ideals onto what is sure to be a foreign cultural context. Were we willing to truly walk a mile within a different culture, it is possible that we might view a practice such as polygamy from a completely different perspective, understanding the benefits gained by those practices within that particular cultural context. Sympathy is limited in its ability to facilitate cross-cultural understanding because it maintains our cross-cultural blinders, fuels defensiveness, and promotes insensitivity to difference.

Empathy can serve as a cross cultural bridge. Effectively empathizing with others means that we must strive to understand their context, priorities, values, and the cultural meanings they assign to events, objects, norms, and practices. This understanding is only achieved by using the effective communication skills we addressed earlier in this workshop—active listening, inquiry, balanced advocacy, and reflection. True empathy requires that we temporarily suppress our own biases, preconceptions, and cultural representations so that we might fully explore those of others.

> " When our beliefs fall under attack by others, we seek validation.
> —Anonymous "

When we couple empathy with **validation**—expressing understanding and more importantly, acceptance of others' cultural worldviews—we wield powerful tools for social change and intercultural effectiveness. It is important to understand that validation of

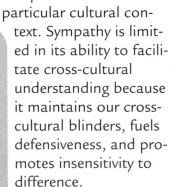

It's probably not empathy if it sounds like . . .

➤ "I know, I'm . . ."

➤ "That happened to me!"

➤ "I once . . ."

➤ "A friend/family member/colleague of mine experienced the same . . ."

➤ "Everybody feels . . ."

➤ "No one enjoys . . ."

others does not diminish the legitimacy of your own cultural perspective, nor does it require apology on behalf of your culture. Validation simply communicates acceptance of the other individual's way of life as relevant *within his or her cultural context*. It provides a refreshing change from the bias and ethnocentrism others who may be different from us generally encounter, and is, therefore, a powerful tool for building mutual trust and respect.

Activity 4.3

Sample Statements of Validation

➤ "I can now understand why you would feel that way, given your history."

➤ "I can only begin to understand the complexity of the situation, given your experience."

➤ "Your ongoing experience with bias sounds very painful."

➤ "Given what you've just shared, I imagine that the differences in our cultures must feel somewhat disconcerting."

Interactive Group Activity: Communication Styles and Preferences

Part A

Determine your answers to the following questions: What communication practices do you find most difficult or frustrating and why? What do you expect from others when you communicate with them?

_____

_____

_____

Part B

Working together with one to three other people, discuss your responses to the above questions. Collaborate in the identification of various cultural origins for the different styles of communication discussed.

Part C

Review this activity by reflecting on the following questions:

➤ Was this a challenging exercise for you? Reflect on your SWOT analysis in Activity 4.1 and comment on your performance in this exercise.

_____

_____

_____

➤ Were your weaknesses apparent in your communication efforts during this activity?

_____

_____

➤ How did your strengths influence the communication process?

_____

_____

_____

➤ How did paying attention and making a concerted effort to utilize effective communication practices influence the quality of the dialogue?

_____

_____

_____

_____

➤ Which skills might you want to continue to attend to and enhance going forward?

_____

_____

_____

TIP:

During Part B, practice active listening, effective inquiry, advocacy, reflection, empathy, and validation. In addition, pay particular attention to the nonverbals guiding your interpretation of others, as well as those you may be using to communicate your own position.

GUIDING PRINCIPLES

It is one thing to conceptually understand what we *should* do in an intercultural context. It is quite another to reprogram our thinking well enough that we actually do them, and do so with little effort. Developing effective communication skills (general and intercultural) requires attention, desire, a comfort with uncertainty, and sometimes, just a willingness to be open to feedback. Workshop 5 expands on this workshop's discussion and explores the intercultural conversation.

Whether you are already advanced in your intercultural communication skills or just getting underway, below is a list of ten guiding principles that are sure to be helpful in creating a positive foundation for all of your interactions going forward. Firmly incorporating these into your existing mental models can support the development of effective communication and interpersonal skills, particularly in an intercultural context.

Principles of Intercultural Communication

1. Every person is unique and should be treated as an individual.

2. Every person has something to offer and his/her own unique brand of wisdom.

3. Every person's behavior is logical within the context of his/her world.

4. Every person's behavior is a result of many complex cultural influences, and can never be attributed to any one thing.

5. Every person has a right to label himself/herself as they wish.

6. Every person has a right to honor his/her history and culture.

7. Every person has a right to be respected and valued; undervaluing, oppressing, or disrespecting others will result in psychological and societal challenges.

8. Every person has a right to seek comfort in familiar faces and customs.

9. Every person has a right to express his/her fears, concerns, and frustrations.

10. Every person has a right to just be different.

Online Research—Using Keywords

For additional resources and information on effective intercultural communication practices, use the following keywords to search online: constructive communication, cross culture communication, effective communication, and intercultural communication.

A few organizations working to build effective intercultural communication practices are the American Communication Association; the Intercultural Communication Institute; and the Society for Intercultural Education, Training, and Research.

Points to Remember

➤ Effective communication has been defined as the art and technique of using words and nonverbals to impart and/or exchange information or ideas.

➤ Communicating effectively, particularly in an intercultural context, requires an emphasis on active listening, inquiry, advocacy, and reflection.

➤ Nonverbals, comprising 80 to 90 percent of what gets communicated, present particularly challenging pitfalls in an intercultural context, given that meanings attributed to common gestures, symbols, and other nonverbal events vary widely across cultures.

➤ Empathy and validation are critical intercultural communication tools and should not be confused with sympathy or agreement.

Endnotes

1. *The American Heritage Dictionary of the English Language*, Fourth Edition, Houghton Mifflin Company, 2000

2. Ibid.

3. P.M. Senge, A. Kleiner, C. Roberts, R.B. Ross, & B.J. Smith, *The Fifth Discipline Fieldbook: Strategies and Tools for Building a Learning Organization*, Doubleday, 1994

4. Milton J. Bennett, ed., *Basic Concepts of Intercultural Communication: Selected Readings*, Intercultural Press, Inc., 1998

5. Ibid.

MAKING CONVERSATIONS WORK

Intercultural conversations are increasingly a workplace reality.

A Conversation Sketch

[Five sales staff—four young men and one young woman—all sit at their desks. They appear to be quite busy with their work, except for one young man, Andy, who seems to be daydreaming as he leans back in his chair and stares at the ceiling. The boss, Mr. Thompson, enters and heads straight for Janet, the woman seated at her desk.]

Mr. Thompson: Janet, would you please meet me in my office in five minutes?

Janet: [Expressing some hesitation as she looks down at her sheet full of possible new leads.] Uh, sure.

[Ten minutes later, Janet sits waiting for Mr. Thompson. She checks her watch impatiently for the fifth time and hopes he isn't going to ask that she perform some silly task he obviously thinks only women should be asked to do. After all, her goal is to be top salesperson this month and these time-consuming, mindless tasks are posing a serious threat. Finally, Mr. Thompson enters and shuts the door behind him. He is getting on in years. Janet swears he moves a little slower today than he did just yesterday.]

Mr. Thompson: Janet, I want you to type up a letter to—

Janet: [Interrupting] You want me to *type* something for you?

Mr. Thompson: Yes, that's right. A letter to—

Janet: [About to explode.] Mr. Thompson. No disrespect, but you've been asking me all week to type things for you. Why don't you ask someone else, one of the guys, for once?

Mr. Thompson: [Looking clearly exasperated.] If you can't handle your workload, why don't you just ask the new guy, Andy, for help?

Janet: Mr. Thompson, why don't you just hire a secretary?

Mr. Thompson: [Feeling somewhat hurt, Mr. Thompson pauses and thinks about all the recent favors he'd done for Janet, a young, single mom. He had allowed her to leave early to pick up her kid, take last-minute personal days, and come in late on several occasions. Now, feeling angry about her apparent lack of appreciation, he decides to assert his authority.] Listen Janet, last time I checked, I was the boss, and as the boss, I'm just asking you to type a letter. This is a team environment, and I need some real players around here. Now, you can either type the letter, or you can choose to not be a team player. Your choice.

Janet: [Looking defeated, she sighs and after a long pause simply nods in resignation.]

Mr. Thompson: Now, I want a letter to John Dennis . . .

GOALS:

Upon completion of this Workshop, the reader will:

➤ Expand on the previous lesson on effective communication skills in an exploration of conversations

➤ Examine the dynamics of collaborative versus "monologue" conversations

➤ Identify the challenges that are unique to intercultural conversations

➤ Identify techniques for troubleshooting and transforming difficult conversations

COMMUNICATION VIA CONVERSATION

In Workshop 4, we reviewed the components that when combined, make for effective communication (active listening, inquiry, advocacy, and reflection). In this workshop, we continue to build on those concepts as we examine a common vehicle for our communication efforts: conversations.

The opening vignette provides a brief sketch of a typical workplace scenario. The boss, interested in exercising his authority and accomplishing a goal, approaches an employee and assigns a task. The employee, motivated by personal reasons (in this case, her own performance goals) pushes back. The resulting conversation is a difficult one.

As readers, we are given access to what is said, but more importantly, to key subtext—the silent thoughts, feelings, and assumptions that play a powerful role in driving the conversation, even though they are not verbally shared between the boss and employee. As you work through Workshop 5, refer back to the vignette and apply the new learning and concepts. At the conclusion of this workshop you will have an opportunity to rewrite the vignette and create a more successful outcome—an effective intercultural conversation.

Productive conversations require a collaborative, not a "monologue" approach.

©PHOTODISC COLLECTION/GETTY IMAGES

HOW DO CONVERSATIONS WORK?

> " Most conversations are simply monologues delivered in the presence of witnesses. "
> —Margaret Miller

Ideally, conversations facilitate information sharing/gathering, conflict resolution, greater understanding, and relationship-building. While the American Heritage Dictionary defines *conversation* as "the spoken exchange of thoughts, opinions, and feelings," this definition both captures the simplicity of the concept and a key pitfall—where we often go wrong in our approach to conversation.[1]

Speaker A says, "I want you to type a letter."

Speaker B responds, "I want to go to Tahiti."

According to the dictionary's definition, a conversation has taken place once Speaker B responds with her thoughts, but what, aside from a mere exchange of thoughts, has this conversation achieved?

Effective conversationalists recognize that the goal of conversation is not to simply deliver monologues in the presence of witnesses or even to advocate their own positions. Instead, they aim to build on their ideas and the ideas of others by collaborating in the communication process toward a specific end—be it conflict resolution, learning, relationship-building, or greater mutual understanding. Therefore, I propose a revised definition of *conversation*: a collaborative effort involving the verbal/nonverbal exchange of requests and/or information (including the associated feelings, thoughts, and assumptions) as a means of successfully achieving a specific goal.

> " The true spirit of conversation consists in building on another man's observation, not overturning it. "
>
> —Edward G. Bulwer-Lytton

WHY CONVERSATIONS CAN BE DIFFICULT

We may suddenly find ourselves in the midst of a difficult conversation for any number of reasons. We may suddenly find ourselves being asked to pay money back to someone who lent it to us three months ago, cornered by a mother-in-law who insists on asking personal questions we would rather not answer, or challenged by a colleague with a strong point of view that significantly differs from our own. All of these situations require that we engage in conversations in which our identities, cultural views, and ideas about what is right or wrong may potentially be subject to review. As a result, we experience anxiety.

EACH DIFFICULT CONVERSATION IS REALLY THREE CONVERSATIONS[2]

In studying hundreds of conversations of every kind, authors Stone, Patton, and Heen have discovered that there is an underlying structure to what's going on, and understanding this structure, in itself, is a powerful first step in improving how we deal with these conversations. It turns out that no matter what the subject, our thoughts and feelings fall into the same three categories, or "conversations." And in each of these conversations, we make

predictable errors that distort our thoughts and feelings, and get us into trouble.

1. **The "What Happened?" Conversation.** Most difficult conversations involve disagreement about what has happened or what should happen. Who said what and who did what? Who's right, who meant what, and who's to blame?

2. **The Feelings Conversation.** Every difficult conversation also asks and answers questions about feelings. Are my feelings valid? Appropriate? Should I acknowledge or deny them, put them on the table, or check them at the door? What do I do about the other person's feelings? What if they are angry or hurt? These feelings may not be addressed directly in the conversation, but they leak in anyway.

3. **The Identity Conversation.** This is the conversation we each have with ourselves about what this situation means to us. We conduct an internal debate over whether this means we are competent or incompetent, a good person or bad, worthy of love or unlovable. What impact might it have on our self-image and self-esteem, our future, and our well-being? Our answers to these questions determine in large part whether we feel "balanced" during the conversation or whether we feel off-center and anxious.

Every difficult conversation involves grappling with these Three Conversations, so engaging successfully requires learning to operate effectively in each of the three realms. Managing all three simultaneously may seem hard, but it's easier than facing the consequences of engaging in difficult conversations blindly.

Revisit the opening vignette. Can you identify evidence of the "What Happened?," Feelings, and Identity Conversations (in either internal or expressed dialogue)?

COLLABORATIVE VS. MONOLOGUE APPROACHES TO CONVERSATION

Authors Stone, Patton, and Heen point out that our particular approach to conversation ultimately determines whether or not it will be a productive, or learning experience. Figure 5.1 summarizes both a collaborative and "monologue" approach to the three conversations. The authors label the collaborative approach as a "Learning Conversation" and the "monologue" approach as a "Battle of Messages."

Figure 5.1 Sort Out the Three Conversations[3]		
	A Battle of Messages	A Learning Conversation
The "What Happened?" Conversation Challenge: The situation is more complex than either person can see.	Assumption: I know all I need to know to understand what happened. Goal: Persuade them I'm right.	Assumption: Each of us is bringing different information and perceptions to the table; there are likely to be important things that each of us doesn't know. Goal: Explore each other's stories: how we understand the situation and why.
	Assumption: I know what they intended. Goal: Let them know what they did was wrong.	Assumption: I know what I intended, and the impact their actions had on me. I don't and can't know what's in their head. Goal: Share the impact on me, and find out what they were thinking. Also find out what impact I'm having on them.
	Assumption: It's all their fault. (Or, it's all my fault.) Goal: Get them to admit blame and take responsibility for making amends.	Assumption: We have probably *both* contributed to this mess. Goal: Understand the contribution system: how our actions interact to produce this result.
The Feelings Conversation Challenge: The situation is emotionally charged.	Assumption: Feelings are irrelevant and wouldn't be helpful to share. (Or, my feelings are their fault and they need to hear about them.) Goal: Avoid talking about feelings. (Or, let 'em have it!)	Assumption: Feelings are the heart of the situation. Feelings are usually complex. I may have to dig a bit to understand my feelings. Goal: Address feelings (mine and theirs) without judgments or attribution. Acknowledge feelings before problem-solving.

Figure 5.1 Sort Out the Three Conversations (continued)

	A Battle of Messages	A Learning Conversation
The Identity Conversation **Challenge:** The situation threatens our identity.	**Assumption:** I'm competent or incompetent, good or bad, lovable or unlovable. There is no in-between. **Goal:** Protect my all-or-nothing self-image.	**Assumption:** There may be a lot at stake psychologically for both of us. Each of us is complex, neither of us is perfect. **Goal:** Understand the identity issues on the line for each of us. Build a more complex self-image to maintain my balance better.

Source: "Sort Out the Three Conversations," from DIFFICULT CONVERSATIONS by Douglas Stone, Bruce M. Patton, and Sheila Heen, copyright © 1999 by Douglas Stone, Bruce M. Patton, and Sheila Heen. Used by permission of Viking Penguin, a division of Penguin Group (USA) Inc.

CULTURE AND EMOTIONS

> " Engaging in a difficult conversation without talking about feelings is like staging an opera without the music. You'll get the plot but miss the point. "
>
> —Stone, Patton, and Heen

Although feelings are an important part of conversations, widely varying cultural norms resulting in a range of comfort levels in addressing emotions make this a particularly difficult area to navigate in the intercultural context. For example, feelings are seldom directly addressed in American conversation, and yet they nonetheless remain a silent but powerful part of the picture, influencing what and how messages are conveyed. Challenges to productive conversations often stem from the dominant American cultural tendency to work hard at appearing "rational." Not only do Americans avoid emotional discussions, but we also tend to avoid discussions *about* emotions as well, particularly in the workplace. Our attempts to appear rational often mean

Where do you fall on the Affective Hierarchy?[5]

Scholar and researcher L. Kibby has captured emotional development on an **Affective Hierarchy**. Progression requires consistently greater insight, reflection, and self-understanding.

➢ **Emoting**—The first step, involving exhibition of emotions

➢ **Emotional Awareness**—Represents development of the ability to label emotions with words or connect emotion to language

➢ **Emotional Intelligence**—Represents the ability to connect emotion with thought: the ability to describe emotions, to see them in context, and to take ownership of one's responses to emotions

➢ **Emotional Agility**—Refers to the ability to move through emotional stages until one reaches an authentic resolution. It enables goal achievement through the development of new perspectives and beliefs, by challenging irrational thoughts/beliefs, and by removing values and beliefs that are triggering or causing emotional distress.

➢ **Self-Noeticism**—The top of the hierarchy is represented by the ability to resolve emotional states based on values aligned with one's genuine self even in those instances when the resultant choices garner disfavor with others

that we engage in internal dialogue that denies or negates our emotions, that we fail at communicating key emotions to others, and that we miss opportunities to create deeper understanding.

Charmaine Härtel, a thought leader and researcher on the subject of emotions, diversity, and organizational effectiveness, supports the importance of realizing the "Feelings" conversation when she notes "individuals and groups require effective emotions communication to achieve and maintain emotional and social health."[4]

CULTURE AND CONVERSATION

The three conversations—the "What Happened?" Conversation, the Feelings Conversation, and the Identity Conversation—are certainly reflected in intercultural conversations. However, research on diversity and intercultural dynamics suggests that the intercultural conversation also incorporates two additional conversations that are unique to this particular context. These are:

➤ The Group Labeling Conversation

➤ The Power Conversation

We must learn to identify and express our authentic emotions.

happy   sad

feelings

angry or mad

embarassed

scared

Similar to the Identity and Feelings conversations, these are often unspoken, and yet they have very strong effects on the dynamics of the intercultural conversation. A brief description of each is provided in the following paragraphs.

The **Group Labeling Conversation** attempts to categorize individuals and render the unfamiliar, more familiar. **Social Identity Theory** states that group members establish a positive social identity for themselves and show favoritism to members of their own social groups.[6] In addition, members hold negative views of those who are different, therefore, individuals are likely to cooperate with in-group members and compete against and exclude out-group members.[7] The **similarity attraction paradigm** indicates that interpersonal attraction and liking is heightened by similarities in attributes, values, and demographic variables such as race, ethnicity, and gender.[8] Accordingly, challenges to productive conversations stem from an "us versus them" perspective, a demonstrated value or preference for those who are similar to us in thought and appearance, an assumption that "different is bad or less than," and a reliance on group stereotypes that results in a "you people" perspective and blinds one or both participants to the *individuals* present in the conversation.

For example, an American having a conversation with a Muslim colleague about politics and religion might, given current world events, find himself relying on stereotypes of a radical Muslim minority and therefore adopting an "us versus them" perspective in conversation.

Individuals from ethnicities and races not belonging to dominant social groups tend to have a keen ear for Group Labeling Conversations. Cues may come from articulated assumptions that fail to hold true for the individual (e.g., a Latin American who does not work in a low-level job and yet is assumed to). At times, however, the cue is blatant use of the term "you people" followed by a stereotype.

Group Labeling Conversations do three things to minimize conversation effectiveness: 1) they evoke a defensive response in the other individual's internal identity conversation, 2) they may elicit negative emotions and challenge the other individual to articulate them, and 3) they destroy the collaborative nature of the learning conversation.

Revisit the opening vignette. Can you identify evidence of the Group Labeling Conversation?

The **Power Conversation** assesses social status and informs conversation and interpersonal protocol. **Social stratification** is defined as "a system of structured social inequality in which groups receive different amounts of the society's wealth, power, and prestige and are hierarchically arranged accordingly."[9] Group rank is determined by the degree to which it differs from the dominant group in culture and physical appearance.[10] Although few Americans will verbally address social hierarchy in conversation, most are, without ever having been shown a graphic representation, able to describe the hierarchy—the order in which racial, ethnic, class, occupational, and other groups fall. One of the first people to propose a model of stratification was Max Weber, who also indicated that groups are aware of differences between themselves and other status groups.[11] Evidence of this awareness comes from the overwhelming homogeneity in club memberships, residential and school clusters, and in what we perceive to be "acceptable" marriage partners. Accordingly, challenges to productive conversations stem from an "Are you worthy of my attention?/Am I worthy of your attention?" perspective, which may determine the type and amount of information we are willing to share, the degree to which we are willing to become engaged or to engage others in conversation, the amount of eye contact we make, our willingness to challenge/be challenged, and our gestures and body language.

Power Conversations do three things to minimize conversation effectiveness: 1) they evoke a defensive response in individuals with lower social status, 2) they minimize the openness or willingness of the individual with higher social status to learn from the other, and 3) they threaten the collaborative nature of the learning conversation.

Revisit the opening vignette. Can you identify evidence of the Power Conversation?

Figure 5.2 summarizes different approaches to the two intercultural conversations.

Figure 5.2 The Intercultural Conversations		
	An Ineffective Approach	An Effective Approach
The Group Labeling Conversation **Challenge:** The situation compels us to confront our fear of discomfort with different social groups.	**Assumption:** I know about you people. You people are the same. You share the same ideas and values. "I'm right, you're wrong" becomes "You people are bad. My people are good." **Goal:** Prove you fit my stereotypes and assumptions.	**Assumption:** We both have inherited many social stereotypes, but we must recognize that every person is an individual. In recognition of possible cultural differences, I must seek to understand what this particular individual feels, values, and believes. **Goal:** Understand both cultural perspectives and how they may truly compare/contrast with each other.

Figure 5.2 The Intercultural Conversations (continued)

	An Ineffective Approach	An Effective Approach
The Power Conversation **Challenge:** The situation threatens our beliefs about equality, fairness, and social progress.	**Assumption:** I'm higher or lower on the social hierarchy, and I expect others to behave accordingly. **Goal:** Maintain the existing social order.	**Assumption:** Social hierarchies exist and are wittingly or unwittingly perpetuated by each of us individually and collectively. **Goal:** Understand the power issues present for both of us. Build a more complex self-image that does not rely on my current power status.

Difficult Conversation Assessment

Think back on a difficult intercultural conversation you may have had recently. Using Figures 5.1 and 5.2 as a starting point, summarize the details as best you can into the five conversations discussed in this Workshop.

The What Happened Conversation

My Assumptions:	My Goal:	What I said:

The Feelings Conversation

My Assumptions:	My Goal:	What I said:

The Identity Conversation

My Assumptions:	My Goal:	What I said:

Activity 5.1

The Group Labeling Conversation

My Assumptions:	My Goal:	What I said:

The Power Conversation

My Assumptions:	My Goal:	What I said:

➤ Reflect on your responses. Did your contributions support a "Learning Conversation" or "A Battle of Messages"?

_____
_____
_____

➤ How might your assumptions and contributions have shifted to support more of a Learning Conversation?

_____
_____
_____

➤ In Workshop 3, we discussed how cultural upbringing plays a significant role in shaping our beliefs about how the world works—our mental models. Think about your personal mental models regarding difference, cultures, and stereotypes and identify your personal challenges in intercultural conversation. How might the mental models and stereotypes you hold interfere with an intercultural learning conversation?

_____
_____
_____

Awareness is key, but practice builds strength and skill.

TROUBLESHOOTING AND TRANSFORMING DIFFICULT CONVERSATIONS

Although we may recognize that intercultural conversations present unique challenges given our preference for others who appear and think like us, few of us ever purposely intend to place ourselves squarely into a difficult conversation.

The following questions will help you to troubleshoot a difficult conversation—one that is not achieving its intended goal (e.g., to gather or share information, resolve an issue, negotiate, or gain agreement).

➤ Are you and the other participants clear about the goal/purpose of the conversation? Is it to solicit information, share information, make a decision, plan a course of action, or something else?

➤ What are you contributing to the conversation? To the immediate challenge?

➤ Are you accepting accountability for creating and checking for understanding?

➤ Are you open to and actively sharing your emotions, thought processes, and assumptions?

➤ Are you questioning the source of your perspectives, ideas, and emotions and open to having them challenged?

➤ Are you demonstrating a willingness to explore and understand the other individual's perspectives, ideas, and emotions?

➤ Are you utilizing effective communication skills: inquiry, reflection, advocacy, and active listening?

➤ Are you reflecting on the dynamics of the conversation and pacing yourself accordingly?

➤ Are you reflecting on your body language and other nonverbal behavior that might be conveying messages to others? Are your nonverbals consistent with a collaborative approach to conversation?

➤ Are you adequately tuning into and addressing the five conversations (What Happened?, Feelings, Identity, Group Labeling, Power) either internally or verbally as appropriate?

Interactive Group Activity: Drafting a Learning Conversation

Part A
Revisit the opening vignette. Was this a Learning Conversation or a Battle of Messages? Was it an effective conversation?

_____

_____

Part B

➤ Identify key intervention points—specific places in the dialogue where a shift might have occurred and resulted in a more productive conversation.

_____

_____

➤ Working together with one to three other people, determine how the dialogue might be rewritten to support a

learning conversation—one resulting in greater understanding between the two individuals. You may refer to the troubleshooting tips in the previous section to support your efforts.

➤ Rewrite and perform both the old and new sketches.

Part C
Debrief this activity by reflecting on the following questions:

➤ Was this a challenging exercise for you? If it was, what was the most challenging part?

_____

_____

Activity 5.2

➤ After you performed both sketches, what was most notable about the old sketch? How did it feel?

_____

_____

➤ After you performed both sketches, what was most notable about the new sketch? How did it feel?

_____

_____

➤ Which of the five conversations did you address in your revised sketch and why?

_____

_____

MOVING FORWARD

By now, you are probably beginning to encounter a few themes regarding your particular cultural perspectives, mental models, communication style, and approach to individuals from different cultures. While the exercises are designed to support exploration of the themes and concepts presented in this workbook, there is no greater learning than that which can be achieved through real-life experience. If you haven't done so yet, increasing your exposure to and seeking out interactions with individuals who may differ from you along one or more cultural dimensions is a great way to practice and hone the skills presented in this workbook.

Workshop 6 will continue to build on intercultural communication skills and support you in the development of constructive feedback skills.

Online Research—Using Keywords

Additional resources and information on making conversations work can be accessed with the following online search terms: art of conversation, learning conversations, communication and conversation, and difficult conversations.

Points to Remember

➤ A balanced use of key communication skills (active listening, inquiry, advocacy, and reflection) is essential for productive conversations, particularly intercultural learning conversations.

➤ "Learning Conversations" require a collaborative approach. Unfortunately, many conversations can be classified as "A Battle of Messages" because people often approach them in an "I'm right; you're wrong," "feelings don't matter," "I must protect my identity," "us versus them," "I'm better than you/you're better than me" approach.

➤ Intercultural conversations are complex because we value similarity, favor in-groups, and compete with out-groups; we are also aware of power differences that influence our willingness to hear and learn from others.

➤ Presented in this workshop were several questions that support troubleshooting and transforming difficult conversations into intercultural learning conversations.

Endnotes

1. *The American Heritage Dictionary of the English Language*, Fourth Edition, Houghton Mifflin Company, 2000

2. D. Stone, B. Patton, & S. Heen of the Harvard Negotiation Project, *Difficult Conversations: How to Discuss What Matters Most*, Penguin Books, NY, 1999, pp. 7–8. Used by permission of Viking Penguin, a division of Penguin Group (USA) Inc.

3. Ibid., pp. 18–19.

4. C. Härtel, L. Kibby, & M. Pizer, "Intelligent Emotions Management," *Key Issues in Organizational Communication*, D. Tourish & O. Hargie, eds., Routledge, 2003

5. Ibid., "Effective Hierarchy" reproduced with permission.

6. O. B. Ayoko, C. Härtel, G. Fisher, & Y. Fujimoto, "Communication Competence in Cross-Cultural Business Interactions," *Key Issues in Organizational Communication*, D. Tourish & O. Hargie, eds., Routledge, 2003

7. Ibid.

8. Ibid.

9. M. N. Marger, *Race and Ethnic Relations: American and Global Perspectives*, Fourth Edition, Wadsworth Publishing Company: An International Thomson Publishing Company, 1997

10. Ibid.

11. Ibid.

LEARNING THE ART OF CONSTRUCTIVE FEEDBACK

The effective manager knows that constructive feedback is a valuable tool.

Criticism or Constructive Feedback?

Roberto,* after graduating from Columbia University with honors, became the newest addition to the company's management consulting team—a prestigious division known for its highly selective recruiting practices. Soon after joining the company, he learned that he was the only person of color on the team. A true double-edged sword, this awareness served both as a source of great pride and anxiety for Roberto.

While Roberto was initially proud of having "broken the color barrier," he was aware that the human tendency to favor *likeness* and disfavor *difference* meant that his performance would likely be judged on the basis of his ethnic background. In fact, he had heard quite a few rumblings of suspicion his first week. Employees expressed concern over speculation that his presence was a direct result of affirmative action in action.

Roberto understood that he had to serve as a positive example, consistently performing above and beyond in order to prove his capability, especially if he was to succeed in keeping the door open for other people of color. He felt an enormous amount of pressure to not only represent himself, but also his ethnic group whenever he participated in meetings, challenged team decisions, or interfaced with other staff. These pressures resulted in a single-minded intensity and drive that left little room for lighthearted humor and socializing, and while others quickly began to notice that Roberto was indeed intelligent and dedicated, they were also turned off by his style.

Finally, recognizing that Roberto's style had distanced him from the rest of the team, his manager suggested a casual chat over lunch on the one-year anniversary of Roberto's employment. Intending to provide constructive feedback that would help Roberto "relax" and "fit in better," his manager instructed him to "lighten up." He shared the team's perception that Roberto was "too defensive and uptight" and that "few people really wanted to put him onto their projects even though they knew he was a hard worker."

Although the manager had done most of the talking, he ended the meeting believing that Roberto had received the feedback well. Needless to say, he was shocked to learn of Roberto's resignation the following day. The manager never did realize that Roberto had interpreted his feedback as a clear signal that no matter what he achieved, he would never be welcomed as a member of the team. In the end, ineffective intercultural communication and feedback resulted in the organization's loss of a talented employee and Roberto's loss of a great career opportunity.

Roberto is a fictitious character; any resemblance to one such person is coincidental and unintentional.

Upon completion of this Workshop, the reader will:

➤ Understand the difference between criticism and constructive feedback, and recognize the benefits of the latter

➤ Understand the role of constructive feedback in facilitating effective inter-cultural communication

➤ Revisit the importance of mental models, empathy, inquiry, and active listening when delivering constructive feedback

➤ Practice application of a simple model for delivering constructive feedback

©RUBBERBALL/GETTY IMAGES

Criticism is not equivalent to constructive feedback.

FEEDBACK COMES IN MANY FORMS

Frequently, I hear people confess that yes, they should really make an effort to provide others with "constructive criticism," but what they don't realize is that this term is a true oxymoron (a combination of contradictory terms such as "illuminating darkness"). By its very definition, criticism is seldom constructive. Following is a closer look at a few related terms to help clarify why this is so.

Positive Feedback

Whether a simple pat on the back or thumbs-up gesture, **positive feedback** is a supportive verbal or nonverbal response that lets others know they are on the right track and should continue doing whatever they are currently doing. Although thought by some to be less important in day-to-day management, positive feedback has always been and continues to be a powerful leadership tool because it directly influences how employees feel about their boss and working environment. Positive feedback is motivating, reinforcing of valuable behaviors, and

supportive of employee retention and engagement.

Examples of positive feedback include:

➤ "Great job on organizing that event, Joe!"

➤ "Your sales figures have been very impressive this past month, Mary. Keep up the good work!"

Criticism

Criticism, sometimes referred to as negative feedback, is defined as the act of criticizing, especially adversely.[1] Because of its evaluative nature, criticism is often expressed in the form of demoralizing labels, judgments, or accusations. In the workplace environment, criticism is often wittingly or unwittingly hurled at an under-performing employee in an attempt to get him/her to recognize that a problem exists and to do something about it.

Criticism, however, seldom accomplishes what we set out to achieve. In fact, it often creates additional obstacles, in some cases, shutting down communication and destroying any opportunity for shared understanding. For these reasons, criticism can be considered "destructive feedback." There are many other challenges also associated with criticism:

➤ It most often obscures the *real* message—what we really want to highlight in terms of a perceived link between what is said or done and the associated undesirable outcome.

➤ It causes employees—offended by the accompanying label, judgment, or accusation—to shift into a defensive mode in an attempt to refute the negative implication. (As reviewed in Workshop 5, the Identity Conversation can easily become a stumbling block in our attempts to effectively communicate or provide feedback.)

➤ It seldom provides the employee with a specific, actionable alternative.

➤ It seldom paves the way for problem-solving and collaborative discussion.

➤ The employee response is hardly what we expect or hope for—often apathy, frustration, resentment, low morale, and an even lower level of engagement or productivity.

©PHOTODISC/GETTY IMAGES

Employee morale, retention, and engagement suffer from criticism.

Criticism also influences how employees feel about their boss and the working environment, but while positive feedback is motivating, reinforcing, and supportive of employee retention and engagement, criticism is quite the opposite—more commonly associated with increased turnover, apathy, and low morale.

Examples of criticism follow (the associated judgments are underlined):

➤ "That presentation was a <u>disaster</u>, John!"

➤ "You're just <u>not reliable</u>, Sue!"

➤ "I need you to be a more effective manager!" (i.e., "You're <u>ineffective</u>.")

Constructive Feedback

The definition of *constructive* is "serving to improve or advance; helpful."[2] Incorporating this definition then, **constructive feedback** can be viewed as a response that supports exploration of new methods, actions, and behaviors that will ultimately ensure mutually beneficial and better outcomes. When delivered with carefully crafted I-statements—statements that assume personal ownership of objective data and are delivered with the intent to help versus blame, such as "I noticed your absence in the employee lounge this week"—we are better positioned to successfully steer clear of classifications, labels, evaluations, or judgments.

Constructive feedback is effective because it ideally:

➤ Demonstrates accountability via I-statements, rather than heightening paranoia with vague statements such as "Someone said" or "Other people think."

➤ Informs others about the link between behavior and outcomes, rather than judging character or speculating about intention.

➤ Highlights specific examples of expectations or needs not being met.

- Focuses on the here and now and addresses specific, rather than general, issues represented by "You always/never" types of statements.

- Creates a bridge for collaborative communication, presenting the situation as a mutual problem.

- Avoids accusing, labeling, or classifying others.

- Addresses changeable behavior, not inherited traits or characteristics such as skin color and ethnicity.

- Motivates rather than demoralizes.

Constructive feedback, like positive feedback, influences how employees feel about their boss and the working environment—motivating, reinforcing, and supporting a high level of employee retention and engagement. Unlike positive feedback, which addresses behavior that is already meeting expectations, constructive feedback serves as a useful tool for behavior modification, performance enhancement, employee development, and ultimately, relationship-building.

Let's take another look at the examples of criticism we used in the previous section:

- *Criticism*: "That presentation was a <u>disaster</u>, John!"

- *Constructive*: "John, I noticed that you didn't support your key points with research findings as I thought you would. How do you feel about your presentation?"

- *Criticism*: "You're just <u>not reliable</u>, Sue!"

- *Constructive*: "Sue, it was my understanding that you would be here at 10:00, not 11:00. How can we work together to make sure you're able to fully participate in these meetings?"

- *Criticism*: "I need you to be a more effective manager!" (i.e., "You're <u>ineffective</u>.")

- *Constructive*: "I'm aware that the low performers on your team haven't made much progress over the past three months as we planned. Can you shed any light on that?"

Activity 6.1

Feedback Assessment

Part A

- Revisit the opening vignette.

- Review the three types of feedback (positive feedback, criticism, constructive feedback) and determine which type of feedback Roberto's manager provided.

- How did Roberto's manager's feedback help or hurt the situation?

_____

Part B
Reflect on your life over the past few months. Identify a situation where you either shared or wanted to share feedback with someone.

- What was the situation? (What specific expectation did the other person fail to meet?)

_____

- How did you respond?

_____

- If you did not provide constructive feedback then, how might constructive feedback have supported a more positive result?

_____

CONSTRUCTIVE FEEDBACK: A VALUABLE INTERCULTURAL COMMUNICATION TOOL

In Workshops 2 and 3, we discussed the influence of culture on the ways in which we view, interpret, and interact with the world. The complexity of each individual's cultural lens—resulting from a combination of gender, race, ethnicity, class, generation, and a host of other social dimensions—translates into a natural diversity of thought and behavior that is ever present in the workplace. While diversity can prove beneficial to both individuals and organizations, conflicting norms, perspectives, and values are a common by-product of diverse work environments. For this reason, constructive feedback, when used appropriately, becomes an essential intercultural communication tool.

In an intercultural context, appropriate delivery of constructive feedback requires us to not only consider our own expectations, needs, and cultural style, but the expectations, needs and culture styles of others as well. For example, in Workshop 4, we explored high context (e.g., Japanese) versus low context (e.g., American) cultures. If an American manager were to consider the unique needs of an employee from a high context culture (e.g., a preference for indirect feedback as a means of "saving face"), then she might, in the interests of getting both needs met, adopt a more culturally sensitive approach to providing such feedback. Although adopting this empathetic approach may initially feel more challenging because it requires that we temporarily work outside the comfort of our existing mental models and norms, the benefits of greater collaboration and understanding support making the effort.

Online Research— Culture and Constructive Feedback

Conduct online research and write three statements to describe the relationship between "culture" and "constructive feedback." (Note: You may address organizational and/or group cultures.)

Example: Results-oriented, *high performing organizational cultures* support and encourage managers to give *constructive feedback* on an ongoing basis.

Example: *Instructors* (professional culture) recognize that *constructive feedback* is an effective tool for helping their students to learn and grow.

1._____
_____

2._____
_____

3._____
_____

Activity 6.2

PREPARE TO GIVE CONSTRUCTIVE FEEDBACK

Before we even approach someone with the intention of delivering feedback, we must first reflect on the mental models and information shaping our interpretation of the situation.

Revisit Your Mental Models: What Do You Truly Expect/Need/Want?

What are your expectations of others? Are they realistic? For example, a "tough" manager's mental model of new employees may result in the expectation that new hires quickly figure things out on their own, and lead to disappointment when they don't. Revisiting your true expectations, needs, and wants can help you to identify where your own behaviors may lay in stark contrast to the outcomes you seek. Building on the previous example then, if the true goal is to have a high-functioning team, the tough manager may discover that it is his own mental model of new employees that is not serving the team well, and not necessarily the under-performance of a particular individual.

Revisit Your Mental Models: Have You Already Sentenced the Individual?

Has the perception that our needs or expectations are not being met prematurely led to categorization, judgment, labeling, or classification of others? It is common for individuals to approach a feedback situation with their minds already made up about the other person. Usually, this assumes a "you're wrong; I'm right" perspective. This is especially so when the other individual comes from a different cultural background because stereotypes often influence our judgments and classifications of others.

If feedback is to be constructive and collaborative, however, you need to first identify the presence of these patterns of thought and then shift your mind-set to create the space required for the openness that can facilitate collaboration.

Check Your Information: What Is the Real Story?

Along with revisiting your mental models is your responsibility to "check the facts." How much of your feedback is based on objective, observable data? How much is based on feeling, assumption, or other intangibles? Being clear about the facts can help you to approach feedback from a rational, unbiased perspective and avoid the pitfalls of criticism. Be prepared to discuss observable behaviors or actions prompting the feedback when you deliver your feedback.

MAKE YOUR FEEDBACK CONSTRUCTIVE

Once you have worked through the above questions, you will be ready to deliver your feedback. It is important to remember that although you will be initiating the feedback, constructive feedback requires collaborative discussion. It's a two-way street in which empathy, inquiry, and active listening rule communication traffic.

THANCS™ encompasses a framework for the effective delivery of constructive feedback.[3] Reminding us that we should always express appreciation for others, the acronym helps us to deliver motivating feedback, even when it is aimed at correcting, improving, or redirecting behavior. Below is a description of the framework with a look back to the opening vignette. Constructive feedback is:

Timely

➤ Deliver your feedback as soon as you can after identifying the gap between desired outcome and actual results, or witnessing an undesirable behavior.

➤ Remember to keep the conversation focused on the here and now.

In the opening vignette, the boss waited one full year before addressing the issue of Roberto's interpersonal style. What might have been a more effective approach?

Helpful

Ensure the recipient is able to walk away with a clear understanding of:

➤ What is expected (in terms of outcomes or behaviors)

➤ Where exactly he/she may be failing to meet expectations

Do you feel Roberto's boss's feedback was helpful? If not, how might he have provided constructive feedback that was more helpful?

Appropriate

When assessing appropriateness, consider:

➤ Context—Constructive feedback should always allow the employee to "save face," and therefore be delivered in private.

➤ Level—We often hold high expectations of others. Are your expectations in line with the individual's experience, level, or role?

➤ Tone—If you are angry or upset, wait until you can present your information in a calm, rational manner. This will accomplish three things: 1) ensure that your feedback is perceived as much more credible, 2) ensure that you get heard, and 3) enable you to stay focused on the real issue at hand.

Do you feel Roberto's boss's feedback was appropriate? If not, what might he have considered and/or addressed to be sure that his feedback was more constructive?

Never Labeling, Demoralizing, or Accusing

➤ Steer clear of generalizing, judging, or attacking the individual's character.

What labels did Roberto's boss use? What might have been the effect of these labels? What might the *real* message have been?

Collaborative and Culturally Sensitive

➤ Consider and respect cultural differences in your approach.

➤ Approach the situation as a mutual problem or issue.

➤ Ask how together you can ensure the expectation is met in the future.

➤ Make sure to allow sufficient opportunity for the individual to present his/her perspective.

➤ Work together to brainstorm possible solutions.

Do you feel Roberto's boss's approach was collaborative? Was his feedback culturally sensitive? What might he have considered or done differently?

Specific

➤ Be specific about the desired outcome or expectation and compare it to the actual result.

➤ Identify a clear corrective plan of action and follow-up plan.

Was Roberto's boss's feedback specific? If not, what might he have addressed to provide more helpful feedback?

Deliver Constructive Feedback with THANCS™

Make sure your feedback is:

➤ **T**imely

➤ **H**elpful

➤ **A**ppropriate

➤ **N**ever Labeling, Demoralizing, or Accusing

➤ **C**ollaborative and **C**ulturally Sensitive

➤ **S**pecific

Interactive Group Activity: Practicing Constructive Feedback

Part A

Identify a current opportunity to share constructive feedback with someone you know. Ideally, see if you can identify a cross-cultural situation. Consider how you might utilize the THANCS™ framework to address the issue, and jot down a few quick notes about the situation:

➤ My expectation is . . .

_____

➤ But what I get from this individual is . . .

_____

➤ Cultural considerations (in terms of feedback delivery) might include . . .

_____

➤ My feedback will begin with the following I-statement . . .

_____

Part B

Work with one to two other individuals. Share your summary of the situation from

Part A. (Be sure to protect the privacy of the other individual, as appropriate.) Spend a few minutes role-playing with your group and test-driving your feedback.

Part C

Once everyone has had an opportunity to practice delivering constructive feedback, debrief by responding to the following questions:

➤ How might culture play a role in each situation?

_____

➤ How does the THANCS™ approach differ from the way I would normally approach this particular challenge?

_____

➤ How might the framework support achievement of my goal in this situation?

_____

©RUBBERBALL/GETTY IMAGES

Never shy away from constructive feedback; it's helpful to everyone involved.

OVERCOME FEAR AND HESITATION

Many people fear giving constructive feedback. Though this speculation is not supported by any particular survey that I know of, my experience working with managers and teams on performance management issues across a diverse range of organizations informs me that this is true. Consider your own reaction to giving constructive feedback. Is it something you personally enjoy and look forward to?

There are many reasons why we fear giving constructive feedback to others:

➤ Uncertainty about how the other individual will respond

➤ Concern about a negative reaction, whether sadness or anger

➤ Anxiety about retaliatory remarks or negative feedback

➤ A conflict avoidance orientation or fear of confrontation

It turns out that most of our concerns highlight common responses to negative feedback and criticism, however, *not* constructive feedback. In fact, my work with managers and teams has consistently demonstrated that well-developed constructive feedback skills result in happier, more motivated, and more engaged individuals and teams. Most people appreciate constructive feedback that is respectful of their needs, cultural identities, and efforts.

Final Tips on Delivering Constructive Feedback

Building on the idea that "it's all in the delivery," the following are a few final tips on giving constructive feedback:

➤ Make sure you use "I-statements." Rather than generalize, speak from your own perspective and remember that just because it begins with the word *I* doesn't mean it's automatically a constructive statement. For example, "I think you're an idiot" is not a constructive statement, no matter how sweet the tone used to deliver it.

➤ Build a bridge. Ask "How can I support you in making sure that going forward [insert the desired result]?" or "How can we work together to make sure [insert desired result]?"

➤ Remember, practice makes perfect. To develop constructive feedback quickly, make sure to use it in your personal life with friends, family, and others; there is no downside to doing so, and the upside is sure to be better relationships with all of the important people in your life.

➤ Don't underestimate others. Sometimes managers will express concern that an employee is too sensitive, too new, or too inexperienced to hear feedback. Delivered from a place of respect, however, constructive feedback need not challenge or hurt others.

Online Research—Using Keywords

Access additional resources and information with the following online search terms: constructive feedback, criticism, feedback, learning organizations, performance management, and positive feedback.

Points to Remember

➤ Criticism is evaluative and is, therefore, often expressed as judgments or accusations that challenge our attempts to engage in effective communication. Constructive feedback, on the other hand, supports new behaviors, personal and professional development, and achievement of better outcomes.

➤ Diverse work environments frequently experience clashes over values, norms, and perspectives. Constructive feedback, when delivered in a collaborative and culturally sensitive manner, is a valuable intercultural communication tool that can support progress toward shared goals and mutual understanding.

➤ When delivering constructive feedback, it is essential that we revisit our mental models and utilize effective communication skills such as empathy.

➤ As with any skill, practice makes perfect. Use constructive feedback with friends, family, and colleagues as a way to quickly develop competency.

Endnotes

1. *The American Heritage Dictionary of the English Language*, Fourth Edition, Houghton Mifflin Company, 2000

2. Ibid.

3. S. Eckert, "How to Motivate Your Employees," *Long Island Business to Business News*, March 2004, copyright S. Eckert

BRIDGING THROUGH CONFLICT

Conflict can thwart effective intercultural relationship-building.

Conflict in the Cafeteria

Manuela, originally from South America and one of the company cafeteria's most loyal cooks, had been working alongside the same colleagues for many years. A few recent staff changes, however, resulted in new reporting relationships and more importantly, a new boss. Although Manuela liked change and hoped new staff meant fresh ideas, she worried that the promotion her ex-boss had promised her would no longer be granted. Her worries about the staff changes began to grow even more when she realized that things weren't going as smoothly as she had hoped.

Anthony, her new boss, was a proud Italian and a proud chef. Manuela likened his strong style to that of "a bull in a china shop" because his arrival was quickly followed by new policies, new operating and reporting procedures, even more staff changes, and the one thing that disturbed Manuela the most—a change in the climate of the working environment.

That climate ignited one day when Anthony overheard Manuela speaking to one of her new cooks, also of Latin descent, in Spanish. Over the years, Manuela discovered that delivering instructions in Spanish to nonnative Latin employees vastly improved their ability to understand and recall information, thus shortening the amount of time required for training. Anthony, overhearing the use of a foreign language in a shared workspace, became angry and abruptly interrupted Manuela and the new cook. "I don't know what your incompetent ex-boss let you get away with, but foreign languages are not to be used in a shared workspace. This is America!" he blurted out. Embarrassed and feeling the stirrings of resentment, Manuela said nothing.

Anthony walked back to his office, slammed the door, and sat fuming at his overcrowded desk. He couldn't believe the amount of work he had on his plate. Leadership was, in his opinion, taking advantage of him as a new employee. They had set impossible financial and operating goals and communicated clear expectations that he successfully meet them by next quarter. To make matters worse, the ex-boss hadn't kept clear records, so Anthony found himself scrambling to get up to speed. It didn't help that English was a second language for almost half of his staff. As Anthony sat thinking about the challenges ahead, he began to regret ever having taken this job.

GOALS:

Upon completion of this Workshop, the reader will:

➤ Examine his/her mental models regarding conflict and review different kinds of conflict

➤ Explore different approaches to conflict and identify his/her particular conflict style

➤ Understand the complex relationship between culture and conflict, and review four intercultural conflict styles

➤ Identify ways to combine culture awareness and effective communication, empathy, and constructive feedback skills to create a collaborative environment for dialogue and conflict resolution

WHAT IS CONFLICT?

> " Conflict is inevitable, but combat is optional.
> —Anonymous "

Conflict. For many people, this one word immediately conjures up powerful images, associations, and feelings. Take a minute and think about your own mental model for conflict. What images, ideas, and feelings do you associate? Are they positive or negative?

Most Americans will make predominantly negative associations, perhaps believing somewhere deep down that conflict is avoidable and unnecessary, and yet many a scholar, researcher, anthropologist, and philosopher have expressed both the inevitability and opportunities provided by conflict. **Conflict** can be defined as *perceived* incompatibilities, whether real or imagined, in perspectives, wishes, and desires. In short, conflict occurs because no two people can ever completely share the same perspectives, wishes, and desires. Our discussion about the vastly multidimensional nature of culture in Workshop 2 illustrates why this is so.

Researchers Ayoko and Härtel make a critical distinction between **destructive conflict**—to which many refer when they think of conflict due to its damaging, adverse effects for individuals, teams, and organizations—and **constructive conflict**—which can result in innovation, improvements, and other beneficial outcomes.[1] They also highlight two additional kinds of conflict: **task conflict**—pertaining to perceived differences in ideas and other task-oriented issues despite having a shared goal—and **social conflict**—which stems from negative feelings and dislike for other groups and is often driven by stereotypes and prejudices about those

who do not share similar beliefs and values, as was discussed in Workshop 5.[2] The important thing to note about social conflict is that because it often results in our rejection of others, it seldom paves the way for constructive conflict approaches. Instead, it often results in destructive conflict, thus perpetuating the misconception that different beliefs and values should be avoided or met with distrust.

©RUBBERBALL/GETTY IMAGES

There are many different approaches to handling conflict.

If you reflect back on any examples of destructive conflict from your own life experience, you may recognize some of the negative consequences of destructive conflict, which include depleted energy, increased stress and tension, weakened interpersonal relationships, low-performing teams who compromise performance against shared goals, high turnover, low team morale, and alienation of those who are culturally different from the dominant culture.

On the other hand, constructive conflict offers benefits such as stronger interpersonal relationships and greater creativity, innovation, problem-solving, cohesion, morale, and individual and team functioning. However, many of us could benefit from further development in the specific techniques that support constructive conflict resolution.

HOW DO YOU APPROACH CONFLICT?

> Whenever you're in conflict with someone, there is one factor that can make the difference between damaging your relationship and deepening it. That factor is attitude.
>
> —William James

What is your natural response to conflict? Although our communication styles may, in general, be somewhat adaptable, experiences with conflict produce stress and anxiety and cause us to fall back on culturally learned approaches. Following are five typical responses to conflict. Can you identify your natural approach?

If your general response to conflict is to . . .

avoid it altogether, then you have a tendency to steer clear of conflict and hope it will resolve itself. The benefit is that you may relieve yourself of some immediate tension. The disadvantages are that you never really resolve the issue, get your needs or the needs of the other individual met, learn anything new about yourself or others, and miss key opportunities to build stronger relationships. Some cultures are predisposed to this approach and may consider more assertive approaches to be "uncivilized," "too aggressive," or "unschooled." Others who adopt a more assertive approach to conflict may consider this approach to be "the easy way out," "useless," "cold and uncaring," or "postponing the inevitable."

If your general response to conflict is to . . .

give in, then you have a tendency to let others make decisions, downplay your own needs, put yourself last, and hope conflict will go away if you do. The benefit is that you may successfully stave off tension and conflict, at least temporarily. The disadvantages are that you often sacrifice your own needs, wishes, and desires; become easy prey for more aggressive types; and often feel manipulated and resentful as a result of your repeatedly giving in. Some cultural groups advocate this approach and may view more assertive approaches to be "self-serving" or "self-centered." Others who adopt more assertive approaches may consider this approach to be "martyr-like," "passive aggressive," "unmotivated," or "uncaring."

If your general response to conflict is to . . .

compromise, then you tend to try to meet others "halfway" and find "good enough" solutions rather than put too much effort into finding creative, but complete **win-win solutions**—solutions that fully meet the needs of both parties involved. The benefit is quick, if temporary, solutions. The disadvantage is that you often fail to explore, and therefore end up sacrificing some part of your own needs, wishes, and desires. As the other individual is also not completely engaged in exploration of his needs, wishes, and desires, he may also walk away not feeling completely satisfied with the result, thus the solution may be only short-lived. Many wholeheartedly believe this is the best approach available and view other approaches aiming for complete mutual gain to be "a waste of time" or "impossible." Others who adopt more assertive and collaborative approaches may consider this approach to be "somewhat like settling," or "halfhearted."

If your general response to conflict is to . . .

get them to see things my way, then you have a tendency to try to control and dominate others, and believe that your way is most often the right way. The benefit in an organizational context is simple: When others need to do something a particular way, you are able to direct them to do so. In an interpersonal context, however, this common approach is more costly than it is beneficial because it often results in destructive conflict. There is a very important difference between **assertiveness**, where one confidently and clearly states his/her point of view, and **aggressiveness**, where one confronts others in a hostile manner or manipulates others without regard for their emotions in the process of advocating one's own points of view. Some cultures believe this approach communicates leadership, power, and authority and view other approaches as "weak," "unsure," "too involved," or "lacking in confidence." Others who adopt more collaborative approaches may consider this approach to be "over-controlling," or "arrogant."

If your general response to conflict is to . . .

find the best possible solution for everyone involved, then you have a tendency to collaborate in problem-solving

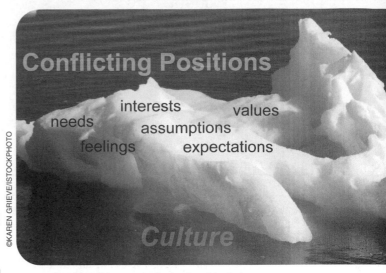

Conflicting Positions

interests   values
needs   assumptions
feelings   expectations

Culture

Conflicting positions are only the tip of the iceberg. Resolution requires navigation through the deeper waters of cultural influence.

and recognize that despite initial perceptions of difference, common ground and shared goals can usually be identified with a little effort. The "disadvantage" is that this approach may be time-consuming because it requires that you dig deep and challenge preconceived ideas. The benefits, however, far outweigh the disadvantages in that this approach enables you to fully explore your needs, wishes, and desires as well as those of the other individual, and build a stronger relationship as both you and the other individual work together to find the right solution. Mediators often adopt this approach, and while a third party may be appropriate in some situations, you yourself can develop the skills that will enable you to facilitate conflict resolution in a collaborative way on your own.

Conflict Personality Assessment

➤ Review the approaches to conflict.

➤ Does any one style capture your general approach to conflict? If so, which one?

➤ Most people tend to adopt different conflict resolution styles in different situations.

1. Consider each style and identify specific conflict situations in which you might be more inclined to use that particular approach.

2. What benefits/disadvantages might be associated with using that particular approach in the situations you identified?

"Avoid it altogether . . ."		
Situation	Pros	Cons
➤ Example: the conflict involves a particular subject such as politics. ➤ ➤	Saves me the stress.	I never get to expand my thinking on the subject.
"Give in . . ."		
Situation	Pros	Cons
➤ ➤ ➤		
"Compromise . . ."		
Situation	Pros	Cons
➤ ➤ ➤		

continued on next page

"Get them to see things my way . . ."		
Situation	Pros	Cons
➤		
➤		
➤		

"Find the best possible solution for everyone involved . . ."		
Situation	Pros	Cons
➤		
➤		
➤		

CULTURE AND CONFLICT

> " Change means movement. Movement means friction. Only in the frictionless vacuum of a nonexistent abstract world can movement or change occur without that abrasive friction of conflict. "
>
> —Saul Alinsky

In Workshop 1, we discussed that the American workplace is increasingly becoming culturally diverse. In Workshop 2, we explored the complexities of culture as well as some of the more salient ways in which cultures differ from one another. If we are unaware of our own culture, each of these key points of difference becomes an ongoing source of potential conflict with others. Only when we understand that our particular perspectives, values, beliefs, and practices are very much rooted in the narrowly defined world of our individual experience can we then open up with a natural curiosity and explore the worlds in which others live. Truly understanding that one way is never "the only right way" to do, believe, or view things can open us up to appreciation for other cultures and the ways in which they have evolved. Unfortunately, too many of us fail to recognize these simple truths, and for this reason, diversity and culture difference remain common sources of destructive conflict in neighborhoods, communities, schools, and organizations.

When we encounter conflict, we tend to believe that we are right and others are wrong, to suspect negative intentions on the part of others, and to become blinded by the other individual's **position**—the particular point of view, stance, or requirement with which we differ. We seldom dig deeper to identify what specific expectations, needs, and values lie beneath these positions, and in an intercultural context, to explore how culture may be playing a role in driving those particular expectations, needs, and values. As a result, we fail to recognize the times when conflict has escalated from such simple intercultural misunderstandings as variations in meaning for a particular word, differences in communication practices, mistakes made by nonnative English speakers who never meant to offend, or differences in norms regarding physical space.

My experience mediating conflict has taught me that it is quite common to encounter individuals with two seemingly opposing positions or points of view who indeed share similar goals and interests. Shared goals and interests are great territory for bridging across difference, but before we even attempt conflict resolution, we must take great care to identify an approach that suits both individuals. The direct approach of many African-Americans, Italians, and Latinos, for example, lies in stark contrast to the East Asian approach, where intermediaries may enable the individuals involved to "save face." Forcing your style onto another individual with different cultural norms will only shut down any opportunity for communication, not to mention conflict resolution and bridging.

Variations of the five conflict styles presented in the previous section have been widely used in workshops, training programs, counseling, and negotiations. More recently however, researchers have begun to question the validity of these styles in a non-Western context. In response, Mitchell Hammer has developed an Intercultural Conflict Style Inventory, briefly outlined in the following sidebar, which identifies four conflict styles used by individuals across many different cultures. Its applicability to cross-culture contexts makes it an exciting, new approach to training on conflict resolution.

Online Research— Exploring Cultural Approaches to Conflict

Choose two specific cultures and conduct an online search to identify norms regarding approaches to conflict for these groups (e.g., Chinese + culture, approach to conflict). Provide a brief description of your findings.

Culture 1: _____

_____

Culture 2: _____

_____

©PHOTODISC/GETTY IMAGES

Developing our skills and awareness of culture can help us bridge through conflict.

Intercultural Conflict Styles[3]

The Intercultural Conflict Style Inventory (ICS), developed by Mitchell R. Hammer, is unique in that it is a cross-culturally applicable tool, a theoretically grounded assessment, and a rigorously validated measure. Inventories, manuals, and additional information can be obtained directly from Hammer Consulting, LLC (www.hammerconsulting.org). A snapshot of the four conflict resolution styles is provided below.

➤ The **Discussion** style emphasizes a verbally direct approach for dealing with disagreements and a more emotionally restrained or controlled manner for communicating with one another. It generally follows the maxim, "Say what you mean and mean what you say."

➤ The **Engagement** style emphasizes a verbally direct and confrontational approach toward resolving conflict that is accompanied by an emotionally expressive demeanor. Disagreements are directly addressed and emotion is "put on the table."

➤ The **Accommodation** style emphasizes an indirect approach for dealing with areas of disagreement and a more emotionally restrained or controlled manner for dealing with each party's emotional response to conflict. Indirect speech, use of stories and metaphors, reliance on third-party intermediaries, and minimizing the level of conflict present among the parties are all specific Accommodation strategies.

➤ The **Dynamic** style involves the use of indirect strategies for dealing with substantive disagreements coupled with more emotionally intense expression. This style may involve such linguistic devices as hyperbole, repetition of one's message, stories and metaphors, and use of third-party intermediaries.

Strengths (as identified by individuals favoring a particular style) and weaknesses (as perceived by individuals favoring other styles) are summarized in the chart below.

Discussion Conflict Style	**Engagement Conflict Style**
Self-Perceived Strengths:	*Self-Perceived Strengths:*
➤ Confronts problems ➤ Elaborates arguments ➤ Maintains calm atmosphere	➤ Provides detailed explanations, instructions, and information ➤ Expresses opinions ➤ Shows feeling
Weaknesses as Perceived by Other Styles:	*Weaknesses as Perceived by Other Styles:*
➤ Difficulty in reading "between the lines" ➤ Appears logical but unfeeling ➤ Appears uncomfortable with emotional arguments	➤ Appears unconcerned with the views and feelings of others ➤ Appears dominating and rude ➤ Appears uncomfortable with viewpoints that are separated from emotion
Accommodation Conflict Style	**Dynamic Conflict Style**
Self-Perceived Strengths:	*Self-Perceived Strengths:*
➤ Considers alternative meanings to ambiguous messages ➤ Able to control emotional outbursts ➤ Sensitive to feelings of the other party	➤ Uses third parties to gather information and resolve conflicts ➤ Skilled at observing changes in nonverbal behavior ➤ Comfortable with strong emotional displays
Weaknesses as Perceived by Other Styles:	*Weaknesses as Perceived by Other Styles:*
➤ Difficulty in voicing own opinion ➤ Appears uncommitted and dishonest ➤ Difficulty in providing elaborated explanations	➤ Rarely "gets to the point" ➤ Appears unreasonable and devious ➤ Appears "too emotional"

Source: Used with permission of Mitchell R. Hammer, Ph.D., Hammer Consulting

COLLABORATING IN CONFLICT RESOLUTION

> " Conflicts may be the sources of defeat, lost life, and a limitation of our potentiality, but they may also lead to greater depth of living and the birth of more far-reaching unities, which flourish in the tensions that engender them. "
>
> —Karl Jaspers

Collaboration in conflict resolution requires effort, dedication, openness, and skill. Following are seven steps that promote a collaborative environment for constructive conflict resolution.

1. Free yourself from blinding stereotypes/beliefs about "others."

    At the earliest sign of intercultural conflict, the first thing we need to do is break the stereotypes and faulty first impressions that blind and mislead us. We do this by making them conscious, acknowledging their presence, and creating the open mind that will enable us to approach conflict from a collaborative perspective and inquire about the individual standing before us. We must also consider how the perceptions others have of us and our culture might be fueling the conflict.

2. Own your part.

    We must assume accountability for our own role in creating the conflict. Personality types that promote conflict include egotistical, ethnocentric, authoritarian, arrogant, dogmatic, controlling individuals, as well as passive-aggressive or conflict-avoidant types and those who fear uncertainty and difference.

3. Identify an appropriate approach to conflict resolution.

    Consider the cultural differences and norms associated with each approach. Work in a collaborative manner within the constraints of cultural norms so that you do not offend or impose on others.

4. Let go of your position.

    It is essential that we let go of our positions so that we might achieve greater clarity about our needs, interests, and expectations. We must ask ourselves "Why?" and explore the truth that lies beneath. At the same time, we must help others to move past their positions by guiding them through the same process of inquiry.

Managing Emotions During Conflict: Using the ERA Model[4]

➤ **E**mpathic listening, or emotive tone listening, is based on the idea that "using words to label or provide a label to describe an emotional state will make the emotional state conscious, which enables the individual to examine and reflect upon the emotion." In other words, using neutral tone and body language to avoid conveying any judgments, the listener says "You feel . . ." and labels the emotion.

➤ **R**eflective listening commences once agreement about the particular emotion fueling the discussion is achieved. The listener then restates the emotion followed by ". . . because you want to . . ." either leaving it open for the other individual to complete or labeling the goal and checking with the speaker for accuracy. This focus encourages clarification of and attention to the goal.

➤ **A**ction-based communication focuses on goal attainment that will alleviate the emotional intensity. This commences once the speaker agrees with or states the goal that is identified through the reflective phase. The strategy is for the listener to ask questions such as "How will that happen? How would that look for you? How would that work for you?"

5. Use effective communication skills, particularly listening, inquiry, empathy, and constructive feedback.

Active listening, inquiry, empathy, and constructive feedback will become your greatest tools in the conflict-resolution process. Listening for what is said as well as what is not said—the nonverbals, body language, and emotional cues—can reveal hidden messages and facilitate progress toward mutually beneficial solutions. Use of open-ended questions creates space for others to share their points of view and to reflect on the cultural influences associated with them. Empathy builds the trust and respect that is essential for collaboration. Constructive feedback, given its collaborative approach, can support openness and honest communication.

6. Manage and label emotions influencing the process.

Emotions are integral parts of the conflict-resolution process. See the sidebar on "Managing Emotions During Conflict: Using the ERA Model" for a suggested approach.

7. Collaborate in problem-solving.

Work together to brainstorm ideal solutions that will meet the specific needs, interests, and values of all individuals involved. Open yourself up to learning about others, and at the same time, be assertive, not aggressive, in sharing your cultural perspectives with others. Use language that reflects the collaborative nature of the process such as "How might we use our shared interests and common goals to create an optimal solution?" "How can we work together to . . .?" "How might both our needs be met by . . .?"

Interactive Group Activity: Resolving the Cafeteria Conflict

Part A

➤ Review the opening vignette.

➤ What conflict styles might Manuela and Anthony be demonstrating?

_____

_____

➤ Working with one or two other individuals, stage a follow-up discussion where two individuals perform the roles of Manuela and Anthony, utilizing constructive and collaborative conflict resolution techniques. (If there is a third group member, ask him/her to observe and prepare to provide feedback.)

Part B

Discuss the following questions.

➤ What was difficult? Easy?

➤ How does this approach differ from the way you might have naturally responded?

➤ What one or two steps might you want to focus on going forward?

➤ How might you respond to someone who does not utilize these collaborative techniques?

➤ How might you accommodate someone whose culture dictates a less direct approach?

MOVING FORWARD: TRANSCENDING INTERCULTURAL CONFLICT

Transcending intercultural conflict starts with developing awareness of your own cultural approach and taking responsibility for your role in creating conflict. Though conflict may be inevitable, the sidebar ten-point checklist can support you in taking the right steps that will strengthen your skills and help you bridge with others through conflict.

A Ten-Point Checklist for Resolving Intercultural Conflict

❏ 1. Aim to defuse the conflict early on. Don't wait until it escalates.

❏ 2. Identify an appropriate approach to conflict resolution. Seek a skilled intermediary if necessary.

❏ 3. Prevent escalation by utilizing effective communication skills, particularly active listening, inquiry, empathy, and constructive feedback.

❏ 4. Consider the five conversations: create a shared definition of the problem, label the emotions, understand personal implications, examine the role of stereotypes, and examine the influence of power difference.

❏ 5. Clarify your concerns, needs, expectations, goals, interests, and cultural norms.

❏ 6. Inquire about the other person's concerns, needs, expectations, goals, and interests.

❏ 7. Search for common ground and avoid getting stuck in positions.

❏ 8. Collaborate in brainstorming possible solutions together.

❏ 9. Agree on a mutually beneficial solution.

❏ 10. Demonstrate your commitment to understanding and resolving the conflict throughout the process.

Online Research—Using Keywords

Access additional resources and information with the following online search terms: culture, conflict, cross-culture conflict, and intercultural conflict.

Points to Remember

➤ Your mental models regarding conflict influence your approach to conflict resolution. Destructive conflict is disadvantageous to both parties, while constructive conflict enables the realization of mutual gains. Task conflict pertains to idea and task-oriented differences, while social conflict, which leads to destructive conflict, pertains to negative emotions evoked by cultural difference.

➤ Psychologists have identified five common approaches to conflict. This Workshop explored the benefits and disadvantages of each approach:

"avoid it altogether," "give in," "compromise," "get them to see things my way," and "find the best possible solution for everyone involved."

➤ Lack of culture awareness results in increased conflict and focuses on positions rather than interests and needs. The four intercultural conflict resolution styles are the discussion style, the engagement style, the accommodation style, and the dynamic style.

➤ Constructive conflict resolution techniques can pave the way for greater intercultural relationship-building and understanding.

Endnotes

1. O. B. Ayoko & C. Härtel, "Cultural Differences at Work: How Managers Deepen or Lessen the Cross-Racial Divide in Their Workgroups," *Queensland Review*, 7(1), June/July 2000

2. Ibid.

3. M. R. Hammer, *The Intercultural Conflict Style Inventory: Interpretive Guide*, North Potomac, MD: Hammer Consulting, pp. 12–13, 2003

4. C. Härtel, L. Kibby, & M. Pizer, "Intelligent Emotions Management," in D. Tourish & O. Hargie, eds., *Key Issues on Organizational Communication*, Routledge, 2003, "Managing Emotions During Conflict," reproduced with permission.

PLANNING FOR CHANGE AND PERSONAL EVOLUTION

Let go of the old and reach higher.

Out with the Old and In with the New

Marietta left the director's meeting feeling angry. Although she had been a key contributor throughout the new talent recruitment strategy development process, two members on the team—Tom and Bob—had, without her knowing, apparently colluded in their decision to control the presentation. Tom and Bob delivered the entire presentation, never mentioning the contributions made by the two other team members, both female.

Worried that leadership would begin to question her value on the team, Marietta felt her temperature rise even higher when she returned to her office to find Tom and Bob sitting on her desk debating about her role in the next steps. "How typical!" she thought. She was just about to challenge their sexist behavior and give them a piece of her mind when she suddenly realized that "the old Marietta" had once again taken over. Thrown into a conflict situation, she had forgotten all about her newly developed intercultural awareness and communication skills. She quickly recognized that the old style would only contribute to further escalation of conflict, and so she redirected her energy.

Instead of reacting with anger, Marietta paused for a moment to reflect on the situation. She realized that she had made a number of escalating assumptions about Tom and Bob's intentions, and that her assumptions were directly linked to the stereotypes she held about male behavior in the workplace. In fact, her anger did not result from their behavior at all, she realized, but from her assumptions about their behavior.

After taking a deep breath, she decided to approach the situation from a new angle. She decided to employ her inquiry, active listening, and empathy skills so that she might fully understand their perspective by asking herself "What was their objective going into this meeting?" Marietta also wanted to be sure to use an appropriate degree of advocacy, clearly articulating her perspective, needs, and concerns with the male members on her team. Recognizing that practice makes perfect, she decided she would use the conflict resolution techniques she had also recently learned. She remembered the importance of getting beyond positions to uncover the hidden needs, values, and interests of both parties, which often revealed common ground and opportunities for bridging.

Much to Marietta's surprise, the conversation went smoothly. It turned out that Tom and Bob had misunderstood an earlier conversation in which the women expressed reluctance to speak before the leadership team. Thinking they were serving the team in doing so, Tom and Bob decided to take the lead. Their intention was never to isolate the women, and they sincerely apologized for this outcome. Having resolved this temporary glitch, they worked together to determine a strategy for future presentations, and as a unified team, then went about the work of deciding the next steps for the project. Marietta reflected on "the new Marietta style," and decided that it was definitely here to stay.

Upon completion of this Workshop, the reader will:

➤ Explore the nature of change and transition

➤ Assess his/her orientation to learning, change, and development

➤ Create a personal mission statement and plan of action to ensure ongoing development of intercultural skills

➤ Explore options for responding to others who may lack intercultural awareness and communication skills

SHEDDING THE OLD

> " Before you can become a different kind of person, you must let go of the old identity. Before you can learn a new way of doing things, you have to unlearn the old way. "
>
> —William Bridges

Educators suggest that learning has not actually taken place until it is linked to behavior change. The initial reemergence of Marietta's old interpersonal style, despite having learned new techniques, demonstrates a common difficulty faced by many people working to transition away from deeply ingrained approaches toward new constructive, culturally aware approaches. While we may conceptually understand the reasons for and benefits of a new behavior, reprogramming ourselves to automatically demonstrate those behaviors is often a challenge—one requiring a conscious effort until the new behavior becomes more habitual. In support of this theory, educators have defined four stages of learning, which are briefly summarized in the following paragraphs.

Unconscious Incompetence

"I don't know what I don't know" captures the first stage of learning in which individuals are often unaware that they do not have certain information or skills. This stage is marked by an overconfidence that exceeds ability, and is reflected whenever we wonder to ourselves "How hard can it be to water ski . . . golf . . . create a PowerPoint presentation" or any other skill we have yet to attempt. For example, you may have been unaware that you did not really have an understanding of culture until you worked through Workshop 2. It isn't until we attempt an activity or access new information that we may realize how much we do not know.

Conscious Incompetence

"I know what I don't know" captures the new awareness that there is much to be learned. Confidence lessens as we realize that we do not have sufficient information or that we lack skill. This awareness often results in discomfort, but ironically, the greatest benefit of this stage also stems from this same awareness: Once we are aware of what we don't know, we can go about the business of practicing the skills and/or seeking out the specific information that will enable us to build competence. Rather than perceiving our limited ability or knowledge as "failure" or "weakness," we can choose to take a more constructive approach and view it as an opportunity for growth and development.

Conscious Competence

"I know how to go about doing what I want to do well" captures the conceptual grasp that typically precedes mastery. For example, you might learn the steps that constitute tango or salsa, but if you are new to the dances, you will quickly learn that knowing and doing are really two very different things. Therefore, "practice makes perfect" becomes the motto for this stage. Although this stage of learning requires more of a conscious effort, confidence begins to build once again as we begin to experience progress and improvement in our abilities.

Unconscious Competence

"I don't consciously think about how to do what I do well" captures the unconscious nature of mastery. For example, a speaker who is fluent in Italian no longer has to consciously focus on the rules of conjugation, as does a beginner. A professional hockey player no longer has to consciously focus on the specific body posture that will best enable him to skate, as does a beginning skater. On the flip side, however, unconscious competence can create challenges for us because it may cause us to shut out opportunities to refine or update the skills and knowledge we already have.

As you reflect on the knowledge and skills that support intercultural competence, identify your current stage of learning. Where might you fall on the learning continuum? How might you ensure continued development and progression along the learning continuum?

NURTURING THE NEW

> " Chaos results when the world changes faster than people. "
> —Anonymous

Successful navigation through **change**, which is often situational and external, requires that we undergo **transition**—the internal, psychological process we use to come to terms with the new situation.[1] As William Bridges, author of *Managing Transitions: Making the Most of Change*, writes, "Unless *transition* occurs, *change* will not work."[2]

Give yourself space and time to grow in your abilities.

In Workshop 1, we discussed the rapid and extensive changes occurring both in the United States and abroad that are resulting in a global workforce. While such changes are already a given, I contend that the psychological transition required to support success in this new culturally diverse arena is seriously lagging. Many Americans are simply not making the transition to embrace cultural diversity. A combination of factors perpetuates this reluctance. They include: the dominant American perspective, which dictates that other cultures should strive to be like us; the American cultural tendency toward a lack of cultural awareness (our own and that of others); a fear of culture difference; a fear of change; unchallenged, often invisible social hierarchies; over-politicizing of the cultural diversity issue, rather than viewing it as a business and social reality; a general lack of intercultural education; and resistance to learning where there is an attempt to educate.

Successful transition requires letting go of the old American cultural norms and perspectives that prohibit intercultural relationship-building and adopting new perspectives and practices that support cross-cultural effectiveness. As was discussed in Workshop 2, cultures not only have the potential to change, but they often do so successfully from one generation to the next. Navigating transition and nurturing the new means that we must be sure to address each of the following steps summarized on the next page.

1. Take a closer look to identify what it is specifically that we must let go of.

   We must closely examine cultural norms and tendencies to assess how they are serving us collectively now. Are they helping or hurting intercultural relations? We must also ask tough questions such as "How might I be personally vested in the status quo?" and "What loss would a change toward greater appreciation of cultural diversity imply for me personally?" Even if we support and value a specific kind of change, we may still find ourselves mourning the loss of something that we may have believed to be previously beneficial to us (e.g., power, status, influence, comfort).

2. Clearly understand the nature of the change.

   To fully understand the nature of the change, we must understand the reasons behind it, as well as the potential challenges and benefits associated with it. We must also closely examine the specific fears (whether founded or unfounded) that are invoked within us when faced with the prospect of such change.

3. Expect and prepare for a period of uncertainty.

   We must recognize that all transition is accompanied by a period of adjustment, like the Conscious Incompetence phase of learning, where we try on new identities and behaviors that may not immediately fit. As we work through the adjustment period, however, we must nonetheless be willing to create space for new behaviors and identities.

4. Create a personal mission statement and plan of action.

   Personal mission statements have a significant impact on our daily interactions with others because, when well written, they elicit an emotional, motivational response, translate into action, and articulate a clear goal. In drafting our personal mission statement and plan of action, we must be prepared to answer specific questions that will help us map our progress: What specific philosophies and ideas will you incorporate in your interactions with others? What specific behaviors will you try on? Where will you seek support and feedback? How will you gauge your development and success?

5. Be willing to challenge ourselves to experiment, to fail, to rehearse, and to perfect.

   As we successfully navigate transition and skill development, we should invite others to support and challenge us in our growth. At the same time, we should shift our mind-sets and recognize that there is no such thing as "failure," only opportunities presented by indications of a need for further development.

6. Shift away from a "doing" mode and move toward a "being" mode.

   Prevailing American cultural norms indicate that we could all benefit from incorporating a greater degree of reflection in our day-to-day interactions with others. Shifting from a "doing" mode, which tends to be externally focused, and adopting a "being" mode, which is more internally focused, can ensure that who we are *being* throughout our interactions with others aligns with our values and goals and supports our continued development.

Our ability to nurture new behaviors and identities is, in large part, determined by our orientations to change and learning. Activity 8.1 provides a mini-assessment designed to support you in beginning the process of reflecting on your openness to change and ongoing development.

Orientation to Change and Learning Assessment

Please complete the following assessment to identify your orientation to change and learning. Read each statement below and note the extent to which you agree or disagree with it, where 1 = not at all, 2 = somewhat, and 3 = very much so.

_____ 1. I actively seek learning and development on an ongoing basis.

_____ 2. I like to be challenged by new ideas and perspectives.

_____ 3. I do not rely on the perspectives and opinions of others to guide my decision-making.

_____ 4. I view change as an opportunity for growth, rather than a threat.

_____ 5. I tend to challenge the status quo and look for better alternatives.

_____ 6. When I encounter new information, I actively research and study it rather than rely on my existing limited information.

_____ 7. I have identified specific coping strategies to help me manage my response to change.

_____ 8. I can easily let go of the old if the new offers clear benefits.

_____ 9. I am not generally resistant to change.

_____10. I support education about cultural diversity.

_____11. I believe that both individuals and organizations would benefit from greater intercultural competence.

_____12. I would do whatever possible to promote intercultural learning, even if it meant being the lone voice at times.

_____13. I personally would benefit from greater intercultural competence.

_____14. I find intercultural interactions to be challenging, yet stimulating.

If you indicated "somewhat" or "not at all" to any of the above statements, then you might benefit from greater reflection regarding your openness to change, learning, and the development of intercultural skills.

PLANNING FOR GROWTH

> " Life is change. Growth is optional. Choose wisely. "
>
> —Anonymous

To quote Stephen Covey, author of _The 7 Habits of Highly Effective People_, "Change—real change—comes from the inside out. It doesn't come from hacking at the leaves of attitude and behavior with quick fix personality ethic techniques. It comes

©ANTONIO MO/PHOTODISC/GETTY IMAGES

Will the roots of your cultural perspectives allow your intercultural competence to blossom?

from striking at the root—the fabric of our thought, the fundamental, essential paradigms, which give definition to our character and create the lens through which we see the world."[3]

As discussed in the previous section, learning is defined by our ability to take in new information, create new knowledge, and translate it into new action. Only when we open ourselves to revisiting and challenging the root of our beliefs, perspectives, and actions—and examine our cultural lens—can we begin the process of evolving into interculturally competent individuals.

The following are three key action steps we can take on a situational or ongoing basis to ensure that we continually strike at the root—our cultural lens, the real source of our intercultural approach.

1. Examine your cultural lens: Ask, "How do my values support the development of intercultural competence? What assumptions am I making right now about cultural difference? How might preexisting mental models be shaping my experiences with others?"

2. Consider the possibilities: Ask, "If I fully embraced cultural diversity and utilized effective intercultural skills, how might I ideally respond in this situation? What opportunities and/or benefits might I encounter as a result?"

3. Set a daily goal: Ask, "What's my one small step for the day? What specific skill do I want to practice? Is my challenge today to simply listen without forming judgments? Is it to practice inquiry rather than advocacy?"

Online Research— Crafting Your Mission Statement and Transition Action Plan

Part A
Conduct an online search to identify the many different ways individuals and groups are supporting development towards an interculturally competent society. Entering a search on the following will provide a good start: cross-culture, diversity, advocacy, organizations.

Part B
Reflect on your values and personal goals. Using these as a foundation, craft your personal mission statement, using the following guidelines:

➤ Define your *personal strength(s)* (e.g., "Use my empathy skills to . . .").

➤ Begin your mission statement with the specific *action* you wish to take (e.g., "Use my empathy skills to partner with colleagues across cultural boundaries . . .").

➤ Articulate the benefit or desired *outcome* of your goal (e.g., "Use my empathy skills to partner with colleagues across cultural boundaries to improve performance . . .").

➤ Rather than craft a personal mission statement that aims too broadly initially (e.g., "world peace"), ensure that your mission statement is motivating to you by defining a particular *environment you wish to influence* (e.g., "Use my empathy skills to partner with colleagues across cultural boundaries to improve performance within my organization . . .").

Part C

Draft your own action plan for achieving your personal mission statement.

I will demonstrate commitment to my personal mission by . . .		
Action	**Time Frame**	**Source of Development or Support**
1.		
2.		
3.		

SETTING THE EXAMPLE

> " Example is not the main thing in influencing others; it's the only thing. "
>
> —Albert Schweitzer

As a society, we are still debating the wisdom or necessity of developing multicultural programs and intercultural skills. Many who understand the importance of proactively addressing this increasingly inescapable reality are well on their way to developing solid skills, while those who do not, remain stuck—caught in the vicious cycle of outdated mental models, tense intercultural experiences, and ever-increasing fear of diversity and cultural difference. One unfortunate outcome resulting from this gap is the pressure experienced by those who do choose to develop intercultural awareness, sensitivity, and skill to appropriately address and respond to those who do not. A common question asked by workshop participants is "What do I say to people who assume I feel the same way they do because we share the same race, gender, or ethnicity?" The answer is to set an example.

Demonstrating and modeling the same competencies you have developed in the process of developing your own intercultural skills can often be the most powerful way to interact with individuals who believe differently from you. Shifting your mind-set so that you consider the different perspectives as a direct result of cultural difference (whether resulting from class, education level, or other life experiences) may help you to apply the same principles when interacting with these individuals. Employing the use of active listening and inquiry to expose mental models, paraphrasing to provide the opportunity for clarification, and advocacy, to simply state your perspectives, values, and interests are all equally viable and highly useful tools in this context.

Interactive Group Activity:
Intercultural Competence Post-Assessment

Part A

Following is an intercultural competence post-assessment to identify your current level of intercultural competence. Read each statement below and note the extent to which you agree or disagree with it, where 1 = not at all, 2 = somewhat, and 3 = very much so.

_____ 1. I am aware of demographic changes taking place in America and understand the implications for me, my community, and the workplace.

_____ 2. I am aware of the challenges and associated benefits of cultural diversity.

_____ 3. I am always aware of the stereotypes that shape my interactions with others.

_____ 4. I don't draw negative conclusions when others do or see things differently.

_____ 5. I know what culture is and how it influences my particular values and the unique way in which I view and interpret the world.

_____ 6. I have spent time exploring the many facets of my culture and how it differs from others.

_____ 7. I recognize that although someone may look very different from me, it is possible that we share a lot in common.

_____ 8. I am aware that because cultures are complex and multifaceted, I can never assume anything about others.

_____ 9. I always strive to get beyond obvious differences such as ethnicity, race, and gender so that I might build effective intercultural relationships.

_____ 10. I make it a point to learn about other cultures.

_____ 11. When I meet someone from another ethnic group or country, I demonstrate an interest in understanding his/her culture.

_____ 12. I understand my role in facilitating effective intercultural interactions.

_____ 13. I am confident in my abilities to recognize and resolve intercultural conflict.

_____ 14. I recognize that building the skills necessary to engage in intercultural relationships is an ongoing process.

Part B

➤ Working in small groups, review your responses in Part A.

➤ How do your responses in the post-assessment compare to those in the pre-assessment from Workshop 1? How might your responses in Activity 8.1 correlate with any difference or lack of difference between your responses on the pre-assessment and post-assessment?

_____

_____

➤ For statements where you responded "somewhat" or "not at all," how might you want to go about further developing your intercultural skills?

_____

_____

➤ In what area has your greatest learning taken place? How might this shift affect your interactions with others going forward?

_____

_____

FRAMING THE BIG PICTURE

Every day we move closer to the reality of a global village—a colorful tapestry of cultures and perspectives that make this world such an interesting place in which to live. Making this cultural diversity ultimately work for us as individuals and as organizations, however, requires a cultural shift, supported by a psychological transition to an appreciation of the value inherent in culture difference.

Reflect on this for a moment: If you knew that every individual you were to ever meet, regardless of background, had at least one piece of valuable wisdom to offer you, would your approach to individuals from other cultures be different? Might it involve a greater degree of curiosity, respect, and appreciation? What we

©PHOTODISC COLLECTION/GETTY IMAGES

Becoming more intelligent together.

believe about culture difference goes a long way toward shaping our experience with it. How will your cultural lens influence you going forward?

Online Research—Using Keywords

Access additional resources and information with the following online search terms: cross-cultural learning, cross-cultural unity, cultural diversity, diversity, learning orientation, learning stages, managing change, and orientation to change.

Points to Remember

➤ Change is situational and external, while transition is internal and psychological. Change cannot work unless transition occurs. Transition involves the process of letting go, a period of adjustment, and the beginning of something new.

➤ The four phases of learning are Unconscious Incompetence, Conscious Incompetence, Conscious Competence, and Unconscious Competence.

➤ We reviewed steps to a successful transition and created a personal mission statement and plan of action to ensure ongoing development of intercultural skills.

➤ Setting an example and role modeling intercultural skills is the best way to respond to others who lack intercultural awareness and communication skills.

Endnotes

1. W. Bridges, *Managing Transitions: Making the Most of Change*, Perseus Books, Cambridge, MA, Copyright 1991 by William Bridges and Associates, Inc.

2. Ibid.

3. S. R. Covey, *The 7 Habits of Highly Effective People: Powerful Lessons in Personal Change*, A Fireside Book Published by Simon & Shuster, Copyright 1989 by S. R. Covey

Index